"This could be c
everything from love to liberty, sex to sanity. The authors, both
women, do it in a humorous, common-sense, let's get-down-to-the-
grits kind of way."
Patricia Nell Warren, Author of "The Front Runner," "The Beauty
Queen," *and* "One is the Sun." *Los Angeles, California*

"This guide is obviously written from the heart. The tone is gentle
and supportive, a big sister encouraging other lesbians to love and
accept themselves and live a full life, free of fear and shame. This
is a much-needed book, one Stevens wishes had been available
when she was younger and needed advice on how to "make it" in a
predominantly homophobic world. It's not preachy, clinical, or
cynical. It's readable, humorous, and, most important, kind. Plus,
it's chock full of useful information and resources. Hooray for these
courageous women!"
Carole Canton, Atlanta, Georgia

"As a therapist, I am always looking for positive material to
recommend to clients who are just coming out and struggling with
their sexual orientation, or are just curious about issues that may
confront them on their path. *How To Be A Happy Lesbian* is just
such a book. It's funny, informative, and instructive. It answers a
whole host of questions I wondered about when I first came out and
was afraid to ask and did not know where to look. I'm
recommending this to many lesbian clients and to friends—it is a
welcome addition!"
Jane Ferguson, M.A. L.P.C., Hendersonville, North Carolina

"This book has a wonderfully casual and informative style. It
dispels many myths and is packed with information that is pertinent
to young women, especially the chapters on STDs and safer sex.
Tracey Stevens and Katherine Wunder write like the warm and
witty big sisters we all wish we had."
Cara Delaney, R.N., Miami, Florida.

"This book is a comprehensive guide that I highly recommend. As an educator, I am impressed to find that it has a wealth of helpful information for young and old, and those that just want to learn more about living in the world as a lesbian. I have never seen such a well-written, interesting book that addresses a broad range of important issues, including safer sex and STDs, communication, role models, and strategies. There is even a comprehensive review of films. This book is not just meant for lesbians who are coming out—there is useful information for all!"
Mary Kay White, Ed.D., Exercise Physiologist/Health Educator, Brevard, NC.

"Why didn't some smart woman think of this before? I've known several lesbians and bisexuals who could really have used this to help them come out and get traveling on their true path. Tracey Stevens and Kathy Wunder have put together a terrifically informative, encouraging book for all kinds of women."
Robin Smith, Candler, North Carolina

"Going against the grain of society is never easy, and a path that only people with great courage take. Coming out can be frightening, exciting, and difficult in the best of circumstances. For those who have made a decision to face the world head on without apology and choose to live life authentically, this book is for you. The authors have given us a gift with this valuable resource for those taking this big step. No longer do you have to go this path alone without resources. Now you have an abundance of solid information at hand. This is a work whose time has come, and none too soon!"
Pat M., Black Mountain, North Carolina

"I read *How To Be A Happy Lesbian* as I have been coming out, and I feel better equipped to handle how to meet people, communicate with them, and what to do and expect when I find that special someone I want to become intimate with."
Bonnie S., College Student

HOW TO BE A HAPPY LESBIAN
A Coming Out Guide

TRACEY STEVENS
& KATHERINE WUNDER, L.P.C.

AMAZING DREAMS
PUBLISHING

Asheville, North Carolina

How To Be A Happy Lesbian:
A Coming Out Guide

By Tracey Stevens & Katherine Wunder, L.P.C.

Published by:
Amazing Dreams Publishing
Post Office Box 1811
Asheville, NC 28802
orders@amazingdreamspublishing.com
http://www.amazingdreamspublishing.com

Unattributed quotations are by Tracey Stevens or Katherine Wunder.

Editing: Snowden Editorial Services, Bookaneditor.com

Printed in the United States of America

Publisher's Cataloging-in-Publication Data

Stevens, Tracey.
    How to be a happy lesbian : a coming out guide /
Tracey Stevens & Katherine Wunder. -- 1st ed.
    p. cm.
    Includes bibliographical references.
    LCCN 2002107472
    ISBN: 0-9719628-0-4
    1. Lesbians--Life skills guides. 2. Coming out
(Sexual orientation)--Handbooks, manuals, etc.
I. Wunder, Katherine. II. Title.

HQ75.5.S74 2002   306.76'63
                      QBI02-200534

This book is dedicated to all the lesbians, gay men, bisexuals, transgendered people, and everyone else deemed "different" by society who are courageous enough to be who they really are; and to the straight people who are so secure with their own sexuality that they are not threatened to call us their family and friends.

A Note to You, the Reader

This book contains information any woman who is coming out would need to know, and it answers questions like "What is a lesbian?" and "How do you accept yourself if you are a lesbian?" It also includes advice on coming out and where to get help if you need it; the language of being lesbian and how to own those names that you may be called; where to go to meet others who are lesbian and the art of knowing who is and who isn't; lesbian anatomy including illustrations and descriptions of all your most delicate parts; plain talk about safer sex, which contains a list of common sexually transmitted diseases and their symptoms and general treatments; hints on communication skills and the importance of trust; advice on romance and how to love not only your partner's body, but also her heart and mind; pointers on making love including instructions on how to find the spots that please a woman most; plain talk about heterosexism and advice on how to cope in the world today; an up-to-date list of some of the best lesbian films; and a chapter on lesbian and gay role models you may not know about.

If you are a little uncomfortable purchasing this book today, it is also available on the Web. You may purchase the soft cover edition to be sent directly to you, or a downloadable PDF file which you can read in privacy on your computer. There are complete instructions on how to do this at:

www.amazingdreamspublishing.com

About the Authors

Tracey Stevens has written and illustrated stories since grade school. She won "The Daughters of the American Revolution Award" for writing an article on Southern slavery when she was eleven years old. In the early '90s she showed her anti-racism paintings throughout Florida, but since that time she has concentrated on writing. All her novels have themes of equality. A

Tracey, left, and Kathy, right, sitting on their back porch in North Carolina.

survivor of child abuse, she also incorporates these issues in her writing, and says that her one mission in life is to bring the darkness of abuse into the light so that people who read her work will know that they are not alone. Tracey was the director of the Writers' Guild of Western North Carolina for two terms. She works as a graphic designer, and also in the fine arts field. She has a passion for horses, especially Spanish breeds, and credits her Galiceno horse Shane for saving her from her childhood. She lives with her partner, Kathy Wunder, and a house full of animals.

Kathy Wunder grew up in various Southern states, but primarily Florida. In the '60s she and her parents lived in Natchez, Mississippi, and Kathy was greatly influenced by their work in the civil rights movement. She has been involved in the civil rights movement herself. After graduate school in Florida, Kathy joined Floridians United Against Discrimination. This group was fighting the American Family Association in their bid to make changes in the state constitution that would allow discrimination against the GLBT community. Her favorite pastimes include reading, going to movies, listening to music, cooking, and spending time with friends. She lives with Tracey; Phantom (her wolf-hybrid); Baby, Booger, Jessee, Cysco, W.T., Devon, Bilton, and Minky (the wild cats); Angelote De Luna (a Paso Fino stallion); and Mr. Pidge (Tracey's pigeon).

Disclaimer

This book is designed to provide information on being lesbian, with sections on coming out, basic physical anatomy of women, safer sex, sexually transmitted diseases, dealing with society, laws and civil rights, counseling, and role models who are lesbian, gay, or bisexual.

Because of the constantly changing information on some of these subjects, especially safer sex practices, facts on sexually transmitted diseases, and laws and civil rights in the U.S., you are urged to read other available material and learn as much as possible to protect yourself. The authors and Amazing Dreams Publishing shall have neither responsibility nor liability for any person or entity with respect to life choices or decisions made, directly or indirectly, from reading *How To Be A Happy Lesbian: A Coming Out Guide.*

Every effort has been made to make this guide as accurate and complete as possible—at the last moment we updated it to include a much needed section on domestic partner abuse—however, there may be typographical errors or the information may have changed during the prepublication period. Therefore, this book should be used as a general guide, and not the ultimate authority on these subjects. For more information, see the bibliography/resource section in the back of this book.

Amazing Dreams Publishing is not just a company selling books—we are committed to forming a supportive community for lesbian, bi, transgendered, and "straight but not narrow" women. Visit our website for live links to resources including organizations that fight for our rights such as GLAAD, GLSEN, and LAMBDA; or RAINN, which operates America's only national hotline for survivors of sexual assault. We have spent many hours researching the best lesbian-friendly places to find books to help your family and friends understand who you are; videos and safer sex items, chat rooms, mailing lists, and Internet hosting. We also offer free E-cards, designed by and for lesbians, information on how to create your own art, and a future support chat room for women coming out. We invite you to visit us at:

www.amazingdreamspublishing.com

Contents

Acknowledgments

I would like to thank Rachel Blue Hudson, Robin Smith, and Susan Snowden, the goddesses of support and editing; Patricia Nell Warren, for wonderful counsel and much needed encouragement; Tori Amos, for advice on exclamation points and being my most incredible muse; Leslie Bonner, Sandra Sullivan, and Nell Firmender, who held the light steady when I was wandering in my tunnel of darkness; Anne and Al Malatesta, my "adopted parents," who have been my most wonderfully supportive chosen family for many years; my buddy Connie Schuett; my friend Star White Deer; Craig Williamson, who urged me to begin this project and has been a much needed support throughout; the great folks at Common Ground Distributors, who allow me to be who I truly am, along with letting me work a four-day work week so that I could continue writing; the Writers' Guild of Western North Carolina (I guess your old "fearless leader" finally got fearless); my hot-blooded Spanish horse Shane, who still carries me through troubled times on his strong back; Jack, James, and David, who are always "just a step away"; my "mother-in-outlaw," who has always treated me like another daughter; and Kathy, my partner and best friend, who not only helped me create this book, but has stood by me during the long lonely hours of writing my novels as well. To all the wonderful people who have encouraged my dreams no matter what, I am so blessed to have you in my life.

Tracey Stevens

To Tracey, my girlfriend and best friend, who encouraged me through my blocks in writing my chapters. For my mother, who has always been my "Rock of Gibraltar" and my first and longest guiding light, and the rest of my family, who have always loved and supported me no matter what. To my mentor and counselor, Pete Fisher, who was always teaching me and still does even though he is no longer with us. And to all the people who have ever touched my life, for helping me learn what I needed to, whether I wanted to or not, and helping me become the person I am today.

Kathy Wunder

Introduction

Over the last ten years, I have written a series of novels about a lesbian community in a fictional place called Sandstone, Florida. Each book features a different couple in a small group of friends. Most of my heroines grew up in dysfunctional families, and the books tell their stories of becoming strong enough to break the patterns they were born into and develop into strong, happy lesbians.

After reading one of my novels, my mentor Patricia Nell Warren said, "Tracey, if you really want to get the message out, why don't you write a nonfiction book based on your own life and what you have learned?"

At first I was scared. If I wrote a book about my life, I would have to totally come out and be honest about who I really am, not just fictionalize it in a book. After much fear and working through every excuse I could think of, Patricia's suggestion finally made perfect sense to me, and *How To Be A Happy Lesbian: A Coming Out Guide* is the product of that one conversation. This book turned into something far better than I thought it could. Instead of being just a basic "how to cope" book, it blossomed into a manual to help women who are in the process of realizing who they are.

It is written from my own experience of being out of the closet since I was sixteen, along with help from my life partner, Kathy Wunder, who is a licensed professional counselor. Kathy received her master of arts degree in counselor education in 1993 from the University of South Florida, and has been working in the mental health field since 1991. She has worked with adults dealing with crisis situations, relationship and family issues, and sexual orientation. She has also worked with adult children of alcoholics, survivors of emotional and sexual abuse, individuals dealing with substance abuse, people coping with grief, and couples needing counseling. Kathy wrote Chapters 4 and 10. Chapter 4 is all about communication, and Chapter 10 includes sections on what to expect if you want to see a counselor, along with a section for counselors on ways to help their lesbian clients.

I really needed a book like this when I was coming out in a small, prejudiced Southern town, but there was nothing back then, and there really wasn't anything out there that covers all the topics included in this book until now. That is why Kathy and I wrote this little manual, and we hope it will help you on your path. Life is too short to live in fear of yourself. Stand tall and proud and know that there are people who care.

Tracey Stevens
Asheville, NC

Quotations From
Women Who Love(d) Women

The reward for conformity was that everyone
likes you except yourself.
—Rita Mae Brown, *Venus Envy*

Creative minds have always been known
to survive any kind of bad training.
—Anna Freud

I can stand out the war with any man.
—Florence Nightingale

You must do the thing
which you think you cannot do.
—Eleanor Roosevelt

It's pretty clear that the struggle
is to share the planet, rather than divide it.
—Alice Walker

If you do not tell the truth about yourself
you cannot tell it about other people.
—Virginia Woolf

CHAPTER 1

What does it mean to be a lesbian today?

Lesbianism and the connection of heart, mind, body, and soul

Being lesbian can mean many things, but basically it's this: women who love, cherish, and have primary relationships with other women. Now I don't mean we are like innocent friends who have back-rubbin' slumber parties, although many lesbian relationships start out this way, including my first one when I was sixteen. This mirrored love is not a choice but a true way of living which comes from deep within us. This is why I term it "a connection of the body, heart, mind, and soul." Some argue that it's environmental, some say biological, and some say it is the soul's choice. I think that it is a combination of all these things, and that we're predestined to be exactly how we are. I totally believe that I was born this way.

I remember standing in a playpen and being incredibly attracted to Marilyn on *The Munsters* when I was still in training pants. Shows how old I am, right? And some of you may even be thinking "Who is Marilyn and what's *The Munsters?*" If you don't know, it just means I was born in the '60s, and believe me, I'm real happy with how old I am now, because I would never want to go back. I've lived through some crazy stuff and learned enough hard lessons to be able to write it all down, in true hopes that you'll be able to learn a few things that will help you on your path.

All those years ago my soul was first attracted to a nice-looking woman on an old black-and-white console TV, and my heart followed right along. My orientation has never changed, but my mind didn't put a label on it. "Me, queer? No way. I just admire my female friends because I don't have a big sister," I'd say whenever that little question of my sexuality popped into my mind. Sure, I dated guys for a while when I was in my early teens, though I never felt anything for them but friendship. It wasn't until I fell totally and unmistakably in love with my first girlfriend that I really understood myself, and the heart, mind, soul, body connection. My heart was racing, my soul was soaring, my body would become incredibly aroused whenever she touched me, and I sure couldn't stop thinking about her. When I figured out what all those signs meant, it was the happiest day of my life. But that is not always the case when women realize they are lesbian.

Coming out in a nonsupportive environment

For some people, admitting you are lesbian, or coming out, can lead to a very lonely road full of fear and condemnation. This can cause low self-esteem, substance abuse, or self-degradation. It's hard to be different than more than 80 percent of the population, but it can also be totally empowering to stand in your own truth. If you are going through rough times, call a crisis hotline, or contact a women's health center. They are usually listed in the phone book. You may be able to find support groups in your area, which are listed in the local weekly newspapers, or join an on-line lesbian support chat room. If you are unsure of your orientation or feeling like you cannot cope with the realization that you are lesbian, find a good therapist and work through it. You can sometimes luck out and find listings for lesbian-friendly therapists in your local gay newspaper.

Before you make an appointment, be sure to check out Chapter 10 in this book. It's all about what to expect if you've never been in a therapeutic situation, including what you need to do to prepare; choosing a therapist; and types of payment plans, like sliding scale plans that enable you to pay what you can afford. If you have trouble with the idea of going to therapy and believe it's for babies or people who can't hack it, think of this: It's a lot easier to admit you need help than to keep on struggling over and over with the same old problems. If you get to the point where your life is not happy, no matter what you do, then it might be time for professional help. And remember, if you don't like the way a therapist is handling your issues, you have the freedom to choose another.

I think for someone first coming out, the wisest thing to do is use good sense concerning who you tell. It's hard enough to realize something this big without going through the trauma of being rejected by some people you thought were your friends. When the time is right, you will know who to tell, who can handle it, and who will no longer be a part of your life. The bottom line, I have found, is this: If someone really loves you unconditionally, then that person will remain on your side. She may not understand your life and why you would choose to be who you really are, and there may be some rocky roads to trudge across in the relationship, but eventually you will come to an understanding in spite of your differences.

Lesbian, gay, bisexual, straight, and all the in-betweens

There are as many varieties of human beings as there are cereals, and some of us can be viewed as just as flaky. As long as it doesn't involve kids or animals, I could care less what two consenting adults do—whatever floats your boat, or your little woman in the boat!

When you first come out, you may be taunted and called names. I cannot stress how important it is to accept yourself, and in doing this you must also accept the names that some of the uninformed may call you. This is known as "Owning the Words" and it is very empowering. It means that you can say to yourself, while looking in the mirror, "Yeah, I'm a bull-dyke, queer, lez, muff-diver, but so what? I'm also incredibly hot, attractive to the wild babes, and can have better action than 80 percent of all the women of the world!" You could also go on and on about all your wonderful qualities, like making good grades in school, having a great job, being a wonderful parent to your kids or animals, being kind to old people, or making the best chocolate cookies in the nation. Look yourself dead in the eye, and praise yourself for being strong and not believing any crap from anybody with negative opinions about who you truly are. You are the one with skin tough as rubber, so let that icky name-calling stuff slide right off of you.

After practicing "Owning the Words" for a while I received an obscene phone call. Among other things, the guy called me a slut. This cracked me up and amidst my giggling I replied, "It's obvious that you really don't know me, because that is the one word that I'm truly not!" I taunted him with the fact that he wasn't bothering me one little bit, and he got so mad that he hung up on me. Now who won that little confrontation? To this day I'm still smiling about it. Instead of hanging onto the negativity of someone who did not know my heart, I turned it around, and I bet it was a while before he made another obscene phone call.

What I'm basically saying in this section is that no matter what anyone says, always concentrate on your positive qualities. I truly believe the Creator gave us all wonderful gifts, but it's up to us to get off our butts and use them.

For the sake of anyone who needs it, here are some basic definitions for being human in the United States. The slang terms are some of the many colorful words you may need to "own." The slang terms may or may not be who you identify yourself as. Sometimes they are used by gay people, but most of the more derogatory ones are used as verbal abuse by the uninformed.

1. **Lesbian Slang: homosexual, homosensual, gay, family, queer, lez, dyke, bull-dyke, muff-diver, homo, lipstick lez, lesbyterian, lesboneese, butch, fem, wears sensible shoes, lesbo, "Just needs a good man."**
   Women who love women emotionally, physically, and with their souls. Some raise children, live in houses or apartments, work hard, pay taxes, enjoy vacations, have a knowledge of something bigger than themselves (e.g., Goddess, God, Supreme Being, Creator) which may support a purpose for being on the earth.

2. **Gay Slang: homosexual, family, homo, lesbian (and all the lesbian slang) queer, faggot, fag, chocolate-packer, pansy, fairy, light in the loafers**
   Primarily people who love the same sex—women who love women and men who love men. Some people use the term "gay men and lesbians" or "homosexual men and lesbians" when describing the two sexes in our culture. Some gay people raise children, live in houses or apartments, work hard, pay taxes, enjoy vacations, have a knowledge of something bigger than themselves (e.g., God, Goddess, Supreme Being, Creator) which may support a purpose for being on the earth.

3. **Bisexual Slang: bi, homosexual, homo, lez, faggot,**

fag, bull-dyke, chocolate packer, pansy, muff-diver, fairy, queer, dyke, sitting on the fence, confused
People who love both men and women. Some raise children, live in houses or apartments, work hard, pay taxes, enjoy vacations, have a knowledge of something bigger than themselves (e.g., God, Goddess, Supreme Being, Creator) which may support a purpose for being on the earth.

4. **Transsexual Slang: homosexual, homo, lez, fag, faggot, pansy, chocolate-packer, muff-diver, fairy, queer, dyke, sitting on the fence, confused**
People who strongly feel they are the opposite sex. Their bodies do not match who they really are inside. They may or may not live in a homosexual relationship. Some may have full or partial sex reassignment surgery. Some raise children, live in houses or apartments, work hard, pay taxes, enjoy vacations, have a knowledge of something bigger than themselves (e.g., God, Goddess, Supreme Being, Creator) which may support a purpose for being on the earth.

5. **Intersexed Slang: hermaphrodites, half-and-half, hermie, freaks of nature**
People who are born with both sex organs, either inside their body or outside. If surgically corrected too early in life, the child may have a gender identity that does not match his or her body, which is called "gender dysphoria." Many will seek sex reassignment surgery later in life. Some intersexed people raise children, live in houses or apartments, work hard, pay taxes, enjoy vacations, have a knowledge of something bigger than themselves (e.g., God, Goddess, Supreme Being, Creator) which may support a purpose for being on the earth.

6. **Transvestite Slang: cross dresser, homosexual, homo, lez, faggot, fag, chocolate-packer, pansy, fairy, queer, dyke, sitting on the fence, confused**
Straight or gay people who dress as the opposite sex, full- or part-time, primarily for sexual gratification. They do not want a sex change, and approximately 80 percent are straight. Some transvestites raise children, live in houses or apartments, work hard, pay taxes, enjoy vacations, have a knowledge of something bigger than themselves (e.g., God, Goddess, Supreme Being, Creator) which may support a purpose for being on the earth.

7. **Drag Queen Slang: cross-dresser, homosexual, homo, faggot, fag, pansy, fairy, queer, confused**
Gay men who wear women's clothing for entertainment purposes or their own sexual pleasure. Approximately 5 percent of gay men are drag queens, and they do not usually want a sex change. Some drag queens raise children, live in houses or apartments, work hard, pay taxes, enjoy vacations, have a knowledge of something bigger than themselves (e.g., God, Goddess, Supreme Being, Creator) which may support a purpose for being on the earth.

8. **Female Impersonator Slang: cross-dresser, homo, homosexual, faggot, pansy, fairy, queer, confused**
Gay, bi, or straight men who wear women's clothing for entertaining other people. Some female impersonators raise children, live in houses or apartments, work hard, pay taxes, enjoy vacations, have a knowledge of something bigger than themselves (e.g., God, Goddess, Supreme Being, Creator) which may support a purpose for being on the earth.

7

9. **Gender Benders Slang: faggot, fag, pansy, dyke, fairy, queer, confused**

   Men and women who dress in shocking ways for entertainment or to make a statement. An example would be a guy I met in a tiny gay bar in Florida. He was a burly, full-bearded, hairy-backed construction worker who was wearing a yellow sundress and combat boots. Some gender benders raise children, live in houses or apartments, work hard, pay taxes, enjoy vacations, have a knowledge of something bigger than themselves (e.g., God, Goddess, Supreme Being, Creator) which may support a purpose for being on the earth.

10. **She-males Slang: faggot, fag, pansy, fairy, queer, confused**

    Men who have breasts and penises. Some have breast implants. Many work in adult entertainment, and there are magazines, found mostly in pornography stores, devoted to the subject. Some she-males raise children, live in houses or apartments, work hard, pay taxes, enjoy vacations, have a knowledge of something bigger than themselves (e.g., God, Goddess, Supreme Being, Creator) which may support a purpose for being on the earth.

11. **Heterosexual Slang: straight, hetero, hets, breeders**

    People who love the opposite sex. Some straight people raise children, live in houses or apartments, work hard, pay taxes, enjoy vacations, have a knowledge of something bigger than themselves (e.g., God, Goddess, Supreme Being, Creator) which may support a purpose for being on the earth.

Whew! There are a lot of ways to be a human, and there are probably way more than I've listed. The point of all the repeats in the descriptions is that there are many more similarities between us than differences. No matter who we are on the inside, or what color we are on the outside, we're all basically made the same way, with blood that makes us strong, guts to get us through the rough times, and souls which link us back to our true selves. We are all in this world together, and for now it is our only true home. If we don't get over our prejudices, it could eventually lead to the end of our planet. So I say use the gifts you have been graced with, because life is too short to waste a moment in negativity. Always step back and put yourself in someone else's shoes instead of name-calling and being petty.

So how do I recognize who is and who's not?

I don't know how many times I have had a straight person sit right next to me and say "I can spot a queer or a lez from a mile away." This totally cracks me up, and I usually just look at them and ask where their queer glasses are 'cause they sure overlooked me! After a big-eyed stare, they will usually go into all the reasons I could not possibly be gay, and I just sadly shake my head.

What most people don't get is that we are everywhere. We are not some stereotype that their parents warned them about. Granted, some of us are more butch or fem, but then again so are some straight people. If someone claims they are straight and they really have the ability to pick out all kinds of gay people, then I would say that person is either MC (missed their calling) or CC (closet case), and they are using their own Gaydar. (See Chapter 6 for an in-depth discussion concerning MCs and CCs.)

What exactly is Gaydar?

Gaydar is an inherent gift that most lesbian and gay men have. It is the ability to recognize another homo immediately, especially if the person is the same sex that you are. It is like a premonition, except you get it when you see someone or even speak to them on the phone. The other person could be walking up the street, driving a car on the other side of a six-lane highway, or appearing on TV. It is just the internal knowing that someone else is the same as you—you spot it, you got it.

Now whether this ability comes from the mind, the heart, or the soul, is unknown, although I tend to believe it is a soul connection. Like knows like, so if some nasty closet case is pointing a finger at you in the office, you might mention that they have three fingers pointing right back at themselves, and that it certainly takes one to know one, especially with Gaydar.

Not all gay people have a fine-tuned sense of Gaydar. I have one friend who has been with women for twenty years and still has no idea who is and who isn't. A lesbian could walk up and rub her breasts right on Connie, and she still would question if they are or not. For those who are hopelessly Gaydar impaired, it might help to visit some lesbian organizations. At least there you won't be smacked for making a blunder of mistaken identity. It may also help to learn the meaning of the basic gay symbols, which are included in the next section.

Homo bumper stickers on the highway of life

There are many symbols that represent our community today. Some are ancient and some are fairly new, but most are used to help us know that we are not alone.

Several years ago, my partner and I were driving home from Memphis, Tennessee. We were in my Nissan truck, which has a rainbow triangle on the back window. We'd been visiting her grandmother in a nursing home and gotten a late start back. While driving through some pretty desolate areas of Tennessee, I was getting more than a little nervous. The highway seemed full of wild country boys in their big American hunting trucks, sporting shot guns in their back windows. The theme song for *Deliverance* was just starting to surface in my mind when a small foreign car flew by. The driver quickly cut in front of us, then slowed back down to the speed limit. It kind of scared me until I noticed the rainbow flag decal on the rear window, along with a "Hate Is Not a Family Value" sticker on the bumper. The young woman driving looked in the rearview mirror, and her girlfriend turned around and waved. Our little lesbian convoy went all the way across Tennessee like this, even stopping for gas together. We never spoke, just smiled at the security we felt being a little pack of dykes traveling into the Blue Ridge Mountains.

The symbols of being gay and what they mean

Black and Pink Triangles
Some people do not realize that gay men and women were imprisoned in Germany before and during the holocaust. In 1935, Hitler passed a law forbidding any kind of homosexual activities, including fantasies. He did this even though he knew his friend and second in command, Ernst Roehm, was a homosexual. Some 40,000 to 60,000 people were convicted, and their initial sentence usually included castration or some other kind of sterilization. By 1942, Hitler's rise to power had changed the fate of gay people from imprisonment to the death penalty. After Hitler had no further use of Ernst Roehm, he had him executed.

When the concentration camps began, gay people were either moved from prison, or captured and brought in with Jewish people. Lesbians, along with prostitutes, feminists, or anyone who did not conform to the stereotype of wife and mother, were imprisoned for being "antisocial." Everyone had to wear triangles pointing down, which represented what they were. Gay men wore pink triangles, and gay women had to wear black triangles. Criminals wore green triangles, political prisoners wore red, and Jewish people wore two overlapping yellow triangles, which formed the Star of David.

An estimated 220,000 gay people died in the concentration camps. The sad part is that when the war ended and the Jewish survivors were set free, the law concerning gay people was still in effect. After starvation, humiliation, torture, and clinging to their lives, gay people were sent back to prison where they remained for an additional twenty-four years.

The triangles, once a symbol of hate, have been reclaimed and turned into a symbol of strength. When worn with a tip pointing up, they stand for fighting back rather than giving up our power. The pink triangle also stands for the phrase "Never Forget, Never Again."

The Labrys

This double-bladed axe was first used by Amazon women over 8,000 years ago, making it the oldest symbol of the lesbian movement. It was a multiple-use tool, like so many of us are fond of, and was used for clearing the land and in battle. The Labrys was also a symbol used by the Minoans (2900-1350 B.C.), which was primarily a matriarical society. Minoeans worshiped a topless Great Goddess who was often shown holding snakes, a symbol of both agriculture and fertility. Known as the protector of women, paintings of this Goddess feature female women at her feet holding labryses.

When articles were published about the labrys in the early 1970s, the symbol was quickly adopted by lesbians and feminists as a sign of power and strength.

The Lambda

This Greek letter was first used in 1970 by the Gay Activists Alliance of New York. No one I spoke with was sure why this symbol was chosen. Some say it stands for liberation, others say it means unity. Whatever it means, it took off on its own and and was declared a worldwide symbol by the International Gay Rights Congress in 1974.

The Rainbow Flag

This symbol was originally created for the San Francisco Gay and Lesbian Pride parade in 1978. An artist named Gilbert Baker came up with the idea of a flag with eight horizontal stripes, which symbolized the following: hot pink for sexuality, red for life, orange for healing, yellow for the sun, green for nature, blue for art, indigo for harmony, and violet for spirit. Baker and thirty volunteers hand-dyed and stitched the flag, and it was such a big success that the following year it was to be mass produced for the 1979 parade. The hot pink color was not available, so the flag was reduced to seven colors instead of eight. During that year, San Francisco's first openly gay city council member, Harvey Milk, was assassinated. The parade committee decided the rainbow flag's bright colors would help to unite the gay community over this tragedy. To facilitate the flag's separate colors being equal on both sides of the parade route, the indigo stripe was omitted, leaving the six-colored flag we have today.

As years passed, many variations of this flag were created, including the Victory Over AIDS Flag, which is the basic rainbow flag with a black stripe on the bottom; an American flag version, which shows the rainbow colored stripes with the standard star-filled blue rectangle; the rainbow flag with the Lambda sign in the left corner; a triangle with the rainbow flag colors; the Leather Pride Flag, which features a heart in the left upper corner and nine stripes—this flag symbolizes the sexual fetish community; the Bear Pride Flag, which has stripes that run at an angle and a bear's paw print in the left corner. (Bears are gay men who have a lot of hair on the face or body, and they may be a bit burly like a bear.) The flag described here is not the official one of the bears, as most groups have their own symbol.

The rainbow flag also inspired Freedom Rings, which were designed by David Spada. Freedom Rings are made of aluminum and are the same six colors as the flag. They are usually worn as jewelry. Freedom Rings are very popular and so are the newer Freedom Triangles—same meaning, different shape.

The Gender Symbols

These symbols have their origin in Greek and Roman times. The female symbol is a circle with a cross beneath it. It represents Venus, who was known as the Goddess of beauty and love. The male symbol is the circle with an arrow pointing up and to the right. It stands for Mars, the God of war. Now, when either of these symbols is paired it means two people of the same sex together.

The Awareness Ribbon Symbols

The Red Ribbon project was started in 1991 by Paul Jabara and the New York Visual Aids group. This charity group, comprised of artists and designers, started out wearing the ribbons to honor their friends who were dying of AIDS. The ribbon moved into public acceptance when it was worn by Jeremy Irons when he hosted the 1991 Tony Awards. The color of red represents blood and the fact that AIDS is a blood-related disease. This ribbon was inspired by the yellow ribbons used as support for American soldiers fighting in wars overseas.

Other ribbons emulating the AIDS Awareness Ribbon include: a pink ribbon representing Breast Cancer Awareness; a white ribbon representing Gay-Teen Suicide; a blue, red, and black ribbon, with a yellow pi in the middle, which represents Polyamory—a group whose members are romantically involved with more than one person at a time; a green ribbon, which represents environmentalists' protests of the rain forest destruction, and many more. Ribbons have taken off to say the least.

If your Gaydar isn't quite on track yet, look for these symbols of pride on bumper stickers, license plates, window decals, earrings, necklaces, key rings, T-shirts, belt buckles, bracelets, and rings.

Where do I go to meet the lesbian of my dreams?

We are everywhere! I met my first girlfriend in a tenth grade creative writing class. My second one I met through friends in college, and the one I am with now, my life partner, I met in a post office. You just never know where you might meet someone, but here are some examples of lesbian hangouts:

Sports, sports, sports

Most of us love some kind of sport. Volleyball, soccer, basketball, and softball are the biggest team sports that attract wonderfully athletic women of all shapes and sizes. Of course not all of them are gay, so have your Gaydar on full power before you approach your favorite female "jock." Other sports that attract lesbians are tennis, golf also known as "Dykes on Spikes," fishing, swimming, canoeing, hiking, biking, kayaking, track, dirt-biking, water and snow skiing, and horse sports, which I am heavily into, along with any other kind of animal activity which leads to the next section . . .

Animal lovers everywhere

Many lesbians love animals, and you can find lots of us at local dog and horse shows, in veterinarians' offices, or walking Rover down a trail. Look for us at pet stores, pet adoptions, and training clinics. My girlfriend takes T-Touch classes for animals, and has told me that there are several "Family Members" in her group. When we take our dog to the dog park, it is almost like Gay Day at Disney World. One thing you can bet on, when there is an animal event, there are sure to be some lesbians there.

Bars and dance clubs

Bars are bars—lots of smoke and alcohol, but sometimes fun places to be. I've always heard, "You'll never find your true love in a bar," and I have yet to know of anyone who has, but why limit yourself? Have a good time, make some contacts, shoot some pool, and dance the night away. Just play it safe and have a way to get home if you become intoxicated. I've heard of several horror stories of lesbians being harassed by police or homophobes after leaving a bar or dance club, so be careful.

Lesbian clubs and groups

Where I live there are several lesbian clubs, such as the Lesbian Hiking Club, a professional lesbians' club, a singing group, and a couple of lesbian writing groups. Some colleges and universities have lesbian or feminist organizations, or you can contact a local NOW chapter to find out what's going on in your area. These are great places to make friends and meet single women. Everyone usually knows someone who knows someone, so get out and socialize in healthy drug-free environments.

Lesbian chat rooms, e-mail groups, and personal ads

I've spent hours in chat rooms, having a great time with gay people from all over the world and meeting some really nice ones, but I did have a really bad experience with a fellow writer who supposedly committed suicide. The people who knew her on-line were very upset for days, but then we found out that the whole incident was made up. Why she chose to do this, I'm not sure, but it made me realize some things about anonymity, and how easy it is to bluff others when you don't have to look them in the face.

E-mail lists are a wonderful way to have pen pals from all over the world. Most of the lists are divided into sub-categories, so you can always find friendly people with similar interests. See the index for the address of one of the best lesbian e-mail lists on the Web.

I have known four people who have placed personal ads, and all have had bad experiences. Like I said about the bar scene, don't limit yourself. You could find the perfect person who is just too shy to go out. Just be careful when using personals, because you never know who is on the other end of the answering machine. Sometimes personals are used by people who are emotionally unstable and so socially backward that they cannot make friends in a normal way. This has been the experience of my four friends, and all have sworn that they would never do it again. This advice is the same for chat rooms. They can be fun places, but keep your eyes open to what may be going on behind those typed messages.

Grocery stores and bookstores

Hey, we have to eat too! Cruise the all-night grocery store with some friends, and see who's out there acting like they are checking out the tofu chicken breasts, when they are really eyeing you! Got a lesbian/gay bookstore nearby, or how about the homo section in your local big book chain? The women are there, believe me, but before you go on a lesbian scouting party, you may want to check out the next chapter. It's a refresher course on women's bodies.

CHAPTER 2

Body talk and basic lesbian anatomy

What's the use of learning this?

Knowledge is power. If you apply yourself to learning everything you can about a woman's body, then you will have confidence in yourself and your abilities to bring your partner pleasure. If you know what a woman's sometimes subtle responses mean, then you can communicate on a deeper level and have a more satisfying relationship.

People ARE different.

The wonderful thing about being human is that we are all basically the same in structure, yet we are all incredibly different. What makes one person swoon in passion can make another totally disgusted. This is why both verbal and nonverbal communication are so important. In this chapter we will concentrate on basic anatomy and nonverbal, or bodily, communication. Verbal communication will be covered in Chapter 4.

What is bodily communication?

When you get cold, your skin may become covered with goose bumps and you can start to shiver. This is your body communicating, "Hey! It's freezing out here. Either get me a big coat, or let's go in by the fireplace." Your body is talking to you constantly, although many of these messages go unnoticed because they are such common occurrences. For most of us, sex does not happen twenty-four hours a day, which means that during arousal, our body's responses can be easily charted.

So what can a body say?

Pay attention to your own responses when you are beginning to get sexually aroused. What do you feel? Is it a heat wave that starts at your feet and burns through your center? Do you get flushed in the face, or red around your chest and neck? Does your heart start pounding and your respiration increase, or does your clitoris swell up and start to itch? Do your hands perspire or do chills break out over your back? Is your mind full of wonderfully intense images of what you would like to do with her?

These are just a few of the messages your body might whisper—or flat-out yell—when you are in the mood. The key is to be aware of your own messages, and then open yourself up to seeing your partner's.

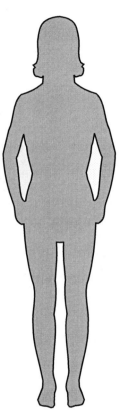

The Lesbian Erogenous Zone (shaded in gray)

Erogenous zones—places that both give you the chills and make you hot

Many people think that erogenous zones are purely genital, but I've found this is far from true. When a lesbian is in the mood, her entire body can be an erogenous zone, and it's up to her partner to learn her favorite places. This can be done by paying close attention to what her body is telling you, or by her actually saying what she likes. Both ways are great, and should be used in conjunction with each other.

Breasts are more than "Got milk?"

Breasts come in all different shapes and sizes. Many women have petite soft mounds, while others have watermelon breasts that are about that solid. Some have huge nipples and some have tiny ones. It's pretty much all up to your own biology what you have sitting atop your chest.

Some women's breasts are extremely sensitive to the touch, even to the point of producing orgasms, while others have boobs of steel, meaning no amount of wonderful stimulation will phase them.

Whatever you have, be proud of them. Even if you could wear your bra backwards and no one would notice, remember the old saying, "More than a mouthful is wasted."

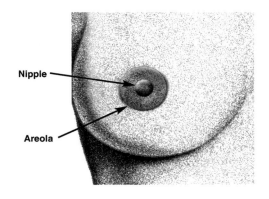

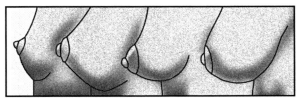

Different breast shapes

21

Introducing the vulva, and I don't mean the car.

Now we are going to get a little technical here, but this stuff is important, so I'll make it as entertaining as possible.

The vulva is composed of all the external parts of a woman's genitals. The whole thing is full of nerve endings, which makes it extremely sensitive to stimulation, so let's start from the outside in.

The Mound of Venus, or mons pubis, is that wonderfully soft pillow that sits atop a woman's pubic bone. It helps pad the area so if your partner is on top of you she won't get hurt. This area can be extremely sensitive in the beginning arousal state for both partners. It is usually covered with pubic hair shaped in an upside-down triangle which points the way to a woman's most magical place.

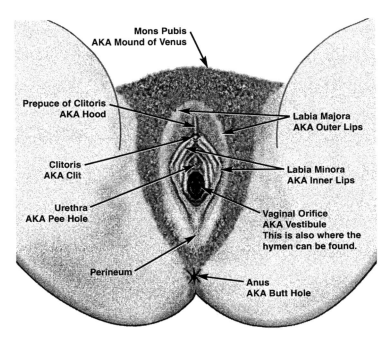

Mons Pubis
AKA Mound of Venus

Prepuce of Clitoris
AKA Hood

Labia Majora
AKA Outer Lips

Clitoris
AKA Clit

Labia Minora
AKA Inner Lips

Urethra
AKA Pee Hole

Vaginal Orifice
AKA Vestibule
This is also where the
hymen can be found.

Perineum

Anus
AKA Butt Hole

As you head down the path of the pointing triangle, you come to the labia majora, or large outer lips. This area consists of two folds of skin covered in hair, and it is also sensitive in the beginning states of arousal. The outer labia is a great place to massage your lover by lightly rubbing the folds together. When you pull them apart, you will find the interior of the vulva.

The labia minora, or inner lips, have no pubic hair. The skin will be similar to your partner's mouth. This area is also a great place to massage (see Chapter 5 for an in-depth description). The two folds of the labia minora meet at the top and form the hood of the clitoris. Also called the prepuce, this skin covers the clitoris.

When stimulation occurs, the clitoris swells and becomes the size of a pea. This area is also known as "the little woman in the boat." The clitoris is the only organ in the whole world whose sole purpose is pleasure. There is nothing else like it in the entire animal kingdom. It is full of nerve endings, and, with the correct kind of stimulation, it can produce as many orgasms as a woman can take. It is sexual perfection at the highest degree and should be celebrated as much as possible.

The urethra, where urine passes through to the outside of the body, is the tiny hole located between your clitoris and your vaginal opening. To help prevent urinary tract infections, always wipe yourself from front to back.

The vaginal orifice, or opening, is also where the hymen is located. The area around the opening, and an inch or so inside, is full of nerve endings. It is a wonderful place to tease your lover (more on that in Chapter 5). The vagina is a muscular, hollow tube which leads to the cervix. The cervix is the entrance to the uterus or womb. Tampons are inserted into the vagina, and babies leave the womb through the vagina.

Leading down to the anus is the perineum. This can be flat, slightly raised, or an actual ridge of skin, like a tiny labia minora. This small area is not that stimulating for most lesbians I've known, although the skin around and in the anus is. The anus should be approached with caution. Some women love to have their anus rubbed; some enjoy penetration into the rectum; and some will totally freak out if you even mention going there. If you or your lover enjoy rectal probing activity, be sure to check out that section in Chapter 5.

CHAPTER 3

Plain talk about safer sex

What is "safer sex"?

Safer sex is a term used to let us know that no sex is the only safe sex. The term "safer sex" comes from the fact that no matter how cautious you are, accidents can happen and there is always a chance of becoming infected with an STD (sexually transmitted disease) when you are intimate with a partner. At this time one in five adults and one in four teenagers have been infected with an STD. Fortunately, there are all sorts of things you can do to help yourself stay healthy and to greatly decrease the possibility of being exposed.

But I thought lesbians couldn't get STDs from each other.

If you think that, then you better cross your legs and pray, because it can happen. There have been cases reported which indicate that lesbians have exposed each other to HIV (human immunodeficiency virus) as well as other types of STDs. Although the number of cases is much lower than other risk groups, it is still way better to be safe than sorry.

Lesbians can be infected with STDs by the following: having unsafe sex with other lesbians or with bisexuals who have been exposed through semen; sharing needles from IV drug use; piercing or tattooing without the proper sterilization techniques; having unsafe sex with men prior to realizing they are lesbian; or having unscreened artificial insemination and/or blood transfusions. Since 1985 blood and semen have been screened at most facilities. Many STDs are transmitted when blood, vaginal fluids (including menstruation), breast milk, or semen from an infected person enters your body or blood stream.

So what can I do to protect myself?

During the time when the acquired immune deficiency syndrome (AIDS) was running totally rampant in the United States, my stepdaughter came to me and asked, "What am I supposed to do, never have sex?" She was dating a new boyfriend she was serious about, and was upset by the media's constant bombardment saying the only way to be safe was to totally abstain from any sexual activity, period. Our little "lesbian family" had also known seventeen people who succumbed to complications of AIDS in six months' time, so we were all pretty paranoid. Because I wasn't in a high-risk group I really didn't know much more than she did, but I did know that STDs have been around probably as long as human beings have, and there are ways to protect yourself from getting them.

When considering intimacy in a new relationship, the first and most important thing is communication. I've known some straight women who were too embarrassed to ask the man they'd just picked up in a bar to wear a condom! I'd look at them and ask "You mean you are willing to get buck naked and screw like a wild dog in heat with a near stranger, but you can't talk about safe sex? Now how crazy is that?" They'd give me all kinds of excuses which essentially boiled down to the old idea that the man knows best. Well, I say that's pure B.S.! Let's not be like some of our straight sisters and let other people decide our destiny. The great thing about being lesbian is that we don't have to play those kinds of games. Most of us know when the other is faking it, so let's not fake safety. When the issue of being together, really together, comes up, then it's up to one of you to bravely broach the subject of safer sex and who's done what.

Now I don't mean you need to rehash every moan you've ever made with lovers of the past, or dig up your most embarrassing sexual moment. But what I do mean is honestly look at your sexual histories and

> **Did you know?**
> In most states, there are laws against not telling your sexual partner if you know that you have a sexually transmitted disease such as HIV, AIDS, syphilis, or hepatitis B. Even if you used safer sex and no infection occurred, you can still be prosecuted for not revealing your status.

ask yourself and each other the following question: In the past five years have you or your partner, or ex-partners, participated in unsafe behaviors listed in the previous section? If so, you may want to have a general blood screening and an AIDS test. Wait 3-6 months after your last risky behavior and have a second test.

Since the virus HIV, which is thought to cause AIDS, can be lingering in your body long before showing up in your blood stream, it is a good idea to abstain from sex or use safer sex practices both six months before and after your AIDS test. Ask your health care professional for the latest information on AIDS, and find out the best way to protect both you and your partner from a potentially deadly virus.

Handy items for safer sex

The way to be the most protected is to make sure that body fluids do not get inside your partner's body or get into her bloodstream via contact. Here are some barriers that will help you in this quest:

Latex gloves

These can be purchased at most drug or medical supply stores. They are essential to use if either partner has a cut or sore on her finger, hand, mouth, vagina, or anus. Using gloves can prevent the passage of a virus into your bloodstream. Some gloves come in designer colors; they can be powdered or non-powdered, and with or without water-based lubricating jellies. Make sure your fingernails are not jagged, which can snag and cut the latex. Gloves are great for all kinds of activities, from clitoral stimulation to vaginal or anal penetration. Make sure to change the gloves between vaginal and anal penetration. (See Chapter 5.)

Finger cots

These little roll-on mini condoms can be purchased at medical supply stores. They are good for clitoral stimulation and some vaginal or rectal penetration. Again, make sure your fingernails are not jagged. If your lover tends to "flood with love," meaning she gets wet enough to almost drown someone, then stick to the full latex gloves. They're much safer.

Dental dams

These five-inch square pieces of latex can be purchased at medical supply stores and come in several colors and flavors. Because unprotected cunnilingus (oral sex) is risky behavior, dental dams of some kind are essential. You can place the whole square over your partner's genitals. You can hold it yourself, or have your partner hold the top while you hold the bottom. Dental dams take a little practice to use safely. Mark the dam with an ink pen to make sure you don't use the wrong side if you happen to put it down, and throw away your dams after one use. If you tend to go out of your head when making love and feel you might not be able to keep track of a dental dam, then single-ply plastic wrap from the grocery store might be better for you. Used the same way as dental dams, plastic wrap can cover her like a big diaper, making wildness safer for everyone. Just make sure you get the non-porous plastic wrap.

If it says microwavable on the box, that is the wrong kind. If you or your partner have trouble feeling stimulus through the barrier, then apply a water-based lubricant to the genital area beneath the dental dam.

Condoms

If you use dildos or dildo shaped vibrators, then latex condoms are a good thing to have around. Instead of having to jump out of the bed to

> **Did You Know?**
>
> Non-silicone dildos and vibrators have porous surfaces that can harbor bacteria or viruses. Even washing them with antibacterial soap may not disinfect them. For non-silicone toys, always use a fresh condom and clean them with antibacterial soap every time you use them for each partner. Silicone is safer because it is nonporous. You can boil a silicone dildo for 5 minutes in water, or wash it with antibacterial soap and hot water, and it will be safe to use without a condom.

wash shared toys, just carefully peel off the used condom and slip on a new one. Make sure to pinch the air out of the end of the condom before rolling it on, because trapped air bubbles can cause a condom to break. You may also want to use a water-based lubricant to reduce friction, which can also cause breakage.

What's considered safe, risky, or unsafe behavior?

Some safe things you can do with your partner are hugging her tightly; massaging her everywhere but there; masturbation (sexually stimulating yourself) or watching her masturbate; phone sex; sharing fantasies; using vibrators or sex toys, but not sharing them without washing or changing the condom; dry kissing which means no tongue action; or tribadism, which means rubbing your body on hers without vaginal fluids, blood, or breast milk exchanged.

Risky behaviors

Heavy French kissing can be risky, especially if you have a sore in your mouth or your gums bleed after brushing or flossing your teeth. Make sure to wait at least 30 minutes before kissing your partner if your gums are the bleeding type.

Shared hand-to-genital contact with finger cots, gloves, or dental dams can be risky if a tear occurs in the latex. Oral sex while using a latex barrier can also be risky if the barrier moves or tears. Inserting your fist into your partner's vagina or rectum, known as fisting, while using a barrier or latex glove is always risky because of the pressure it puts on delicate vaginal or intestinal tissues, which are full of tiny blood vessels. Also, exchanging sex toys without washing them or using fresh condoms, any form of S&M or rough sex that involves piercing or shaving, or any sort of blood letting are very risky behaviors.

Unsafe behaviors

Some totally unsafe behaviors include: oral sex without a barrier, especially during menstruation; ingesting female fluids or ejaculate; sharing dildos or vibrators without a condom or without changing condoms in between users; licking the anal area, or rimming, without a dental dam or plastic wrap; fisting, especially without a glove; any kind of unprotected sex (not using a condom) with a man including oral, vaginal, or anal sex; sharing needles whether for drugs, piercing, or tattooing.

If you use IV drugs, DO NOT share your needles, syringes, or other equipment such as spoons or anything that a contaminated needle may come in contact with! This is very dangerous behavior because minute amounts of blood remain in used needles. In this vacuum state any virus can remain active much longer than when it has been exposed to air.

If you are compelled to use the same equipment for IV drug

use, please sterilize it in the best way possible with bleach. Draw the bleach into the syringe through the needle and then shoot it into the sink. Do this twice. Rinse the entire syringe with uncontaminated water, fill with the water, and shoot through the needle several times to get all the bleach out.

If you and your partner are considering having a child

If you use a sperm bank, make sure that the donors are screened for all kinds of STDs, especially AIDS. If you use sperm donated by a male friend, the old turkey baster routine, make sure he has had at least two negative HIV tests six months apart. The first test should be six months after his last possible exposure to HIV. The next test should be another six months later. In between the two tests and the date he supplies sperm, your donor must have no exposure whatsoever to HIV. This means he would have to be celibate or have been in a long-term, totally monogamous relationship with someone who is also not practicing any risky behaviors, such as IV drug use. At this time, the FDA is in the process of making it more difficult for gay men to donate sperm to sperm banks and to women they already know.

A serious warning

Just like drinking and driving can kill you or others, so can drug or alcohol use prior to or during sex. Your judgment can be impaired to the point of not using safer sex practices. Don't throw away what you've learned in this chapter and use the excuse of "I was too drunk to remember how to do it." Passion is a wonderful thing, but not quite wonderful enough to die for. Worldwide, millions of people have perished from STDs, especially AIDS. Please don't become one of the statistics.

A list of STDs, their symptoms, and general treatments

Chlamydia

Chlamydia is a bacterial disease and is the most common STD in the United States. Chlamydia is a dangerous disease to women because there are few or no symptoms. One to three weeks after exposure, a watery mucus discharge may or may not come from the vagina. There can also be a burning feeling during urination. Chlamydia can cause both pelvic inflammatory disease and sterility. It is usually treated successfully with antibiotics.

Cold sores or fever blisters; clinical name - oral herpes or herpes 1

Cold sores, or fever blisters, are caused by the herpes virus. They can be transmitted by kissing, sharing washcloths or towels, or drinking from the same cup. After the first outbreak, the virus can be dormant for many years. It may reoccur if you are under stress, have a high fever, or are overexposed to the sun. Treatment is usually a prescription cream. Avoid spicy or acidic foods, which may aggravate the condition.

Crabs or cooties; clinical name - pubic lice

Pubic lice are tiny crab-like insects that take up residence in the genital region. The most common symptoms are intense itching caused from their bites, and small dark spots of crab feces left in your underwear. These nasty little critters can be spread by having sex with an infected partner or by coming in contact with contaminated clothing, bedding, or toilet seats. Wash in hot water or dry clean all bedding and clothing that has come in contact with the lice. Treatment is fairly simple with over-the-counter medication.

Genital herpes or herpes 2; clinical name - herpes simplex

Genital herpes is an incurable viral infection. It is spread by sex, and occasionally by fingers that have herpes blisters or sores. Nearly 70 percent of herpes is transmitted through asymptomatic shedding, which means the person infected has no outward symptoms but may still spread the virus. Studies show that at this time almost one-third of sexually active, unmarried adults have herpes. The most common symptoms appear two to ten days after infection and can include swollen glands, a general run-down feeling or flu-like symptoms, and an itching or burning pain in the genital area. Small red bumps will form that can turn into white blistery-looking sores.

The initial symptoms of genital herpes last about three weeks. These symptoms may return and are sometimes caused by stress, but will heal much faster than the onset of the disease. It is most contagious when the symptoms are present, but it can be spread at other times as well. Herpes can cause miscarriage of a pregnancy, and it can be passed on to newborns or cause serious health consequences if open sores are present during childbirth. In these cases a cesarean section will often be preformed. Safer sex practices should always be used if one of the partners has herpes. Treatment for the disease is usually a prescription of an oral antiviral medication. It is important to keep the sores clean by daily washing with soap and water and then carefully drying them.

Genital warts caused by the human papilloma virus (HPV)

Genital warts are caused by a viral infection and are spread through vaginal, anal, and oral intercourse and during childbirth. The most common symptoms are small, reddish, round, possibly itchy bumps which can be inside the vagina, throughout the genital or anal areas, or in the throat. If allowed to grow, the warts can even block openings of the vagina, anus, or throat. Some strains of this virus may increase the risk of cervical cancer. Treatments include chemical or surgical removal, prescription creams, or freezing with liquid nitrogen. Even if genital warts are removed, the virus that causes them is still in the body, which can cause future outbreaks.

Gonorrhea

Gonorrhea is caused by the bacterium *Neisseria gonorrhoea*. It is the oldest known STD, and was mentioned in the writings of Plato. There are few or no symptoms in most women infected, making it a very dangerous disease. If symptoms do occur they are usually within two to ten days after infection and include having a thick, yellowish discharge from the vagina, burning pain when urinating, pelvic inflammation, swelling of the vulva, and possibly arthritic-like pain in the shoulder. In later stages this disease can cause bleeding between periods. Gonorrhea can be spread through any unprotected sexual activity. If left untreated, it may move into your joints resulting in arthritis, cause problems with your heart or central nervous system, or cause pelvic inflammatory disease. It can also blind newborn babies. Treatments for gonorrhea include antibiotics and pain relievers.

Hepatitis B

Hepatitis B is a highly contagious virus spread by unprotected sex, intimate contact such as kissing or using the same toothbrush, and needle-sharing. Nearly one hundred times more infectious than HIV, hepatitis B is the the only sexually transmitted disease that has a vaccine. It seldom has symptoms during the most contagious stages, though symptoms may develop such as fever, nausea or vomiting, fatigue, and loss of appetite. It can cause severe liver damage resulting in death if not diagnosed. No medical cure exists for hepatitis B. It is advisable to stop all drinking of alcohol, stay home and rest if you feel tired, and drink at least eight glasses of water a day.

HIV; clinical name - human immunodeficiency virus

HIV is a virus which may change to the acquired immune deficiency syndrome (AIDS.) First diagnosed in 1981, AIDS has become a disease of epidemic proportions, so far killing an estimated twenty million people worldwide. Linked to infections caused by the human immunodeficiency virus (HIV), AIDS is most commonly spread by sexual contact or IV drug use. It is not caused by casual contact such as shaking hands, hugging, or even drinking out of the same glass.

HIV infection can go undetected for years with few or no symptoms. HIV destroys the infection-fighting white blood cells, gradually wearing down the body until any small cold that is regularly fought off could be almost life-threatening. When the immune system collapses, opportunistic infections develop. Symptoms can be one or several of the following: fatigue or a general sick feeling; fevers, chills and/or night sweats; swollen lymph glands in the back of the neck or armpits; frequent long-lasting colds; weight loss; diarrhea caused by no apparent reason; coughing and general breathing problems; sores that are hard to heal, or the purple lesions called Kaposi's sarcomas.

As of yet, there is no vaccine against AIDS, and the safest sex possible is an absolute must for anyone diagnosed with the disease. There are several treatments available to stabilize a person with symptoms, but at this time no cure is available.

As I said at the beginning of this chapter, AIDS wiped out seventeen of my friends in six months' time, and they were not all gay men either. In other countries AIDS has been primarily a heterosexual disease. I consider it a horrible plague which was not taken seriously by the U.S. government for many years. I'm not sure if the reason was because it was first considered a "homosexual disease" but the bottom line is this: because AIDS was left unchecked in the United States it has spread into all populations. But remember, just because you are carrying the HIV virus does not mean that it will convert to AIDS.

I have known people who have lived with HIV for fifteen years and more. What they say is this: "The best thing to do is to take very good care of yourself, including proper diet, and exercise. You must alleviate all forms of drugs, including drinking and smoking—essentially anything that will wear your immune system down. Make sure to get the right amount of rest, do not over-work or over-stress yourself, and do not constantly dwell on your disease." The last statement, I believe, is one of the most important. If you keep thinking you are going to get sick, your body will follow what your mind is saying, and I know this for a fact.

I had an acquaintance who seemed perfectly healthy. Her sister was a hospice nurse in another state who worked primarily with AIDS-related illnesses. One of her clients turned out to be my friend's ex-boyfriend. Her sister called and told her that her ex was dying of AIDS and that she had better get tested. This was six years after their breakup. My friend had the test and turned out to be positive, and within a few months she was gone from this earth. Her husband, with whom she'd been having unprotected sex for several years, has had many tests since her death, but has never tested positive.

I'm not saying it is better not to know if you are infected with HIV or not, especially if you could risk giving the disease to someone you love. What I am saying is that a positive mental outlook can go a long way in keeping you healthy, not just in the case of AIDS, but in your whole life.

Molluscum contagiosum

Molluscum contagiosum is a fairly harmless infection of the genital area or thighs. Caused by a virus, the symptoms are small, pinkish-white lumps that if squeezed may express a cheesey material. The infection is spread by intimate contact and/or sexual intercourse. It usually will disappear on its own within three to twelve months, or your dermatologist can remove the lumps by freezing, chemicals, or electrical current.

Pelvic inflammatory disease (PID)

Pelvic inflammatory disease is a reproductive system infection that may be caused from other STDs such as gonorrhea or chlamydia. Symptoms can include nausea, chills, fever, vomiting, abdominal pain, spotting between periods, and heavy bleeding or blood clots during menstruation. The best treatment is a combination of antibiotics and rest with no sexual activities.

Syphilis

Syphilis is one of the oldest known STDs and was first seen in fifteenth century Europe. Syphilis is caused by an organism called *Treponema pallidum* and can be passed by kissing and other forms of sexual contact. Syphilis can cause brain damage, and nervous system and heart failure. Symptoms begin ten days to three months after infection and include painless sores that appear on or in the mouth, rectum, or genitals. Second stage syphilis can include fever, sore throat, rash, and patchy hair loss. In the third stage, syphilis attacks the nervous system and can destroy bone and joints and can even lower the blood supply to the brain. Treatment is only effective during the first, second, and symptomless stages and usually involves antibiotics, such as long-acting forms of penicillin.

Trich; clinical name - trichomoniasis

Trichomoniasis is a vaginal infection caused by a parasite. Symptoms begin four to twenty days after exposure and include yellowy-green vaginal discharge with an odor, pain during sex, or painful urination. Treatments include antibiotics and abstaining from sex. Even if one partner is not showing overt symptoms, both should be treated at the same time to prevent reinfection.

Yeast infection or thrush; clinical name - candidiasis

A common yeast infection is caused by the fungus *Candida*. *Candida* is usually present in the mouths, intestines, and vaginas of most healthy women. When the body's acidity changes an overgrowth of candida can cause a yeast infection. Symptoms can include a dry itchy feeling around the vulva; a thick, cottage cheese-like discharge from the vagina that may or may not have a strong odor. This fungus can also affect the throat, tongue, or the lining of the mouth and is then known as thrush. A yeast infection can be spread through sex including oral sex. The best treatments are prescription or over-the-counter antifungal creams or suppositories.

For more info

If you think you may have been exposed to an STD, see a doctor or go to a women's health clinic. You can also contact the National STD/AIDS Hotline at 1-800-227-8922.

The most important thing about STDs is not to be exposed to them. The only way to do this is to be safe and communicate openly with your partner. If you have trouble with communication, be sure to read Chapter 4. It was written by the "Goddess of Communication," my counselor girlfriend, Kathy. She's taught me more about verbal communication than anyone else, which is why I've asked her to write the chapter.

CHAPTER 4

Communication: The key to working relationships

Communication—seems easy—but is it really? The romantic *ideal* is that your partner knows just what to say and knows what you want and need, and you won't have to say a thing. We get this message from movies, TV, and romance novels. The reality is that no one can read our minds, and we can't get mad at our partners if they don't give that hug when we need it or say "I love you" when we want to hear it the most.

The hard part is learning to ask for that hug or those three little words that mean so much. Waiting for your partner to say or do something you want, and her not knowing it, causes hard feelings on your part and leaves your girlfriend wondering what's wrong. It may even get to the point where you give her the silent treatment or become irritable. More than likely, she will then get upset and a fight will start. At some point she may have even asked you what was wrong and you may have told her "nothing." This chapter will help you learn how to communicate more effectively so that the above scenario happens less and smoother communication happens more often.

We all have heard that there are two types of communication: verbal and nonverbal. You never have one without the other. What might be surprising is that nonverbal takes up the largest percentage of communication with verbal coming in a distant second.

The reason for this is that the words are only a small part of communication. The bulk comes from facial expressions and body language. For instance, suppose you run into a friend and ask her how she is doing. She openly smiles and says, "Fine." Her arms are at her sides and they're relaxed. Now you run into another friend and ask the same question. This person smiles tightly, nothing more than a showing of her teeth; her eyebrows are pulled down; her arms are crossed over her chest, and in an angry tone of voice she replies, "Fine!" Would you think your friend was "fine" or would you think the answer was not matching all the other cues given?

We process the nonverbals so automatically we usually don't think about them, we just react to them. There are also those times when we may ask someone how they are and they say "fine" but they seem subdued. Again, a nonverbal and more subtle cue than the circumstance just described, but no less meaningful.

In the circumstance where the verbals don't match the angry nonverbals one would usually ask, "What's wrong?" In the circumstance where the messages don't match and are subtle, we may choose to ask if everything really is all right, or we may leave it alone and take it at face value. The best option here would be to err on the side of caution and ask anyway.

Remember: pay close attention to the verbals and pay even closer attention to the nonverbals.

Basic rules of communication

None of us really learns to communicate effectively. Most of us have poor role models in our parents and other relatives, on TV, and in movies or books. This is a general statement but it applies to many people. We have learned to blame other people for what we feel, and we are taught to put the responsibility on them instead of on us where it belongs.

How often have you heard, or made, these statements? "You made me mad." "You made me feel like an idiot." "You embarrassed me." "You made me happy." Or "You made me excited." The reality is no one can "make" us feel anything without our permission. Our reactions are our own and we react to circumstances or others.

Think of a time when you were driving some place you really didn't want to go, to do something you really didn't want to do. Say someone cut you off in traffic and you got mad. You may have cussed and yelled at the other person through your windshield, shot a bird, or passed and given the other driver a nasty look as you sped by. Now think of a time when a similar circumstance happened and you were in a good mood and looking forward to getting to your destination. Someone cut you off and you just shrugged your shoulders, or maybe you cursed the person under your breath, but you decided you were in too good of a mood to let something so trivial get under your skin; then you focused back on looking forward to getting where you were going.

This is an example of how we are in control and not someone else. It shows how we react to circumstances and how they don't control us. This is the basis of good communication for anyone—accepting responsibility for your feelings.

The following are other basic ground rules to help you and your partner, or you and anyone else, to communicate more effectively. Following them can stop arguments from turning into fights or stop misunderstandings from becoming arguments.

Them's fightin' words!

The basic rules of communication are as follows:

1. Don't use the words "should," "would," "could," "never," or "always." These are all words that are guaranteed to raise the hackles of another person, and the automatic response to one of them is to feel the

need to defend oneself with an angry retort. If you really want to make it a *coup de grace*, point your finger while saying, "You never . . ." or "You should . . ." or use one of the other fightin' words. Those two things together will really push someone into overdrive and a full-scale war could ensue. Another fightin' word to never use is "why?" I learned this the hard way. While I was working on my master's degree one of my instructors had warned us not to use that word too frequently when working with clients. I decided to experiment and asked a client "why" a number of times. Talk about a reaction. People usually respond in an angry manner when asked this because they feel that they are being challenged, not believed, or that their integrity is being questioned. That little experiment was over ten years ago, and I have never repeated it.

2. Don't get into a shouting match. Keep your voice neutral and nonaccusatory. Use a conversational tone and make declarative statements that allow you to take responsibility for your own feelings. Examples of this would be "When you said such-n-such I felt so-n-so." Or "When you did such-n-such, I felt so-n-so." This enables you to take the responsibility for your reaction to the situation without your partner feeling that there is something she needs to defend herself about.

3. Avoid using "but" and "yeah, but." How many times have you either said or heard someone else say something like, "I know I shouldn't say that but . . ."? What this really means is you don't really mean what comes before the "but." Your real intention is what comes after the "but." When someone says "yeah, but" it has the same hidden meaning. For example,

someone gives you some advice you asked for. Your response is "Yeah, but I just can't do that." You have just dismissed the advice you asked for and have given an excuse as to why you don't want to follow that advice. Also remember that when you say "can't" it really means "won't." If someone were to ask you if you could go to the store for them right now and you're busy, you may say, "I can't right now. Maybe later." The true meaning is that you are choosing to follow through with what you are planning, or doing, and so you won't go until later.

4. Agree on your rules for discussion before you ever have your first argument, and agree to stick with the rules. Keep in mind that if the two of you can't agree on something, you may be better off agreeing to disagree on a subject. One of the rules that goes with those listed in this section is to agree that if your voice or your partner's voice becomes angry, or if you both begin to shout or become overly emotional or blaming, then it is time to stop and take a break. This means that if you reach this point, one of you should go to one room and the other one to a different room. One person can go for a walk while her partner soaks in a tub. Anything to separate from each other until everyone has cooled off and both parties are willing to meet back at the discussion table in a calm manner. One of you may notice before the other that things are escalating, so work out a word, phrase or a hand sign to indicate the need for a time out. One of you can use it when needed in the heat of an argument.

5. DO NOT EVER ARGUE IN BED OR GO TO BED IN AN ARGUMENT. If you argue in bed then you can

start equating bed with the place to fight, not with the place of love, safety, and security that it needs to be. If an argument starts in bed, get up and go to another room to have that argument.

6. Allow each person to have her say without interruption. If someone doesn't get to complete a statement and is frequently interrupted, she may get more and more frustrated and begin to feel that what she says doesn't matter.

7. The discussion needs to be kept only to the issue that is the problem. Don't bring up things that happened two weeks, two months, two years, or two decades ago. The issue must be kept to the one that is affecting you and your partner right now. Don't turn it into every issue that you have ever had in your relationship.

8. Choose a time and place to bring up an issue if you are unable to discuss it at the time it occurs, and commit to it. Come to the table with all of your concentration on ways to clear up the problem, and work on leaving chips off your shoulder.

9. Work with your partner to find solid, and if need be, creative solutions to your problem. This may involve alternatives and compromises for both of you. An example may be that if everything turns into an argument then go someplace public to discuss the issue. Or go outside on the lawn to have that argument. The idea here is to put yourselves into a place where neither of you will be raising your voice or escalating.

10. Always start out by giving the other person a positive, or something you really appreciate that your partner

has done. After this is stated, move onto the statements of behaviors that are at issue. Then end with a positive. In other words start with a positive, place the issue in the middle, then end it with a positive. This allows your partner to feel that you are not always picking out bad things about her, and it also allows you to focus on the positive things about your partner.

11. Do not target your partner's sensitive areas. In other words, don't target her with things that you know are going to get her angry and upset. For instance, if she doesn't like the way her mother does something, don't tell her, "You're just like your mother. You take cheap shots the way she does."

12. After you get things resolved to a comfortable place for both of you, make a point to check in with each other to discuss how things are going. You can schedule this or do it on an impromptu basis. Checking in with each other allows you and your partner to fine-tune progress and changes.

13. If you and your partner argue, apologize if you are wrong. Don't give any excuses with your apology. When you do this, it comes across as not taking responsibility for your emotional reaction, not only to your partner, but to yourself as well.

The point of all these rules is to help both you and your partner have a win/win outcome and not a winner/loser result. If you find you have a winner/loser result then someone will feel she has been taken advantage of. If this happens too many times, then hard feelings start to develop.

Arguments are not a bad thing and are not to be avoided at all costs. They are where growth comes from, and a healthy form of communication that can also enhance your relationship.

Coming out

Coming out to others is a personal decision. We have the right to tell those we choose that we're lesbian. By the same token, we do not have the right to tell others that someone else is gay or lesbian. Coming out is an intensely personal experience so a good rule of thumb is, I mind my business and you mind yours.

Each of us must choose if we wish to be in or out of our own personal closets, and to what degree. Some are out to friends and no one else; some are out to friends and family, but not at work; and some are out in all circumstances. It is up to the individual to decide what is right for her/him.

You have to decide how comfortable you are with coming out, and with whom you wish to be out. Do some research on the topic by reading books specifically about the coming out process, and decide what suits you best and what course you wish to follow. There are also books on coming out to your parents (see the bibliography and resource section). If you choose to come out to your parents, it may be helpful to have a book for them in one hand and information on PFLAG (Parents and Friends of Lesbians and Gays) in the other.

PFLAG is a national organization with chapters in cities all over the United States. Their primary function is to serve as a support group for people who have lesbian, gay, or bisexual family and/or friends. There are also lesbians and gays who are members of these groups.

The wonderful thing about PFLAG is that if you want to go and check out a local group before referring your parents or friends there, you can. You can also attend meetings with them. If there is more than one group, you or your parents and/or friends may want to check out all of them. Groups have personalities just like people. You may find that you feel more comfortable with one group than the other. It doesn't mean that one group is better, it just means that you or your parent(s) or friend(s) feel more comfortable with one group than the others. Information about PFLAG, along with other lesbian and gay organizations, is listed in the index at the back of this manual.

Trust

Trust is the most important thing in a relationship. If you don't have trust, you don't really have a relationship. There are a lot of lesbian couples who stay very insular in a bid to protect their relationship. In the long run this does more damage than good. Some couples also give up individual interests and only do things together. This is usually done because there is not always respect for relationships by other lesbians. Someone told me that a woman who was a friend of her partner's actually came up to her at a party and said, "If you two ever break up, let me know. I'd be interested."

The point here is that you may run into situations where someone else is approaching you, or your partner, and expressing a sexual interest. This is where the trust comes in. If it's you, just handle it in a calm and firm manner. Let the other person know that you are in a committed relationship, and that you are not interested. If someone is flirting with your partner, or your partner tells you that someone has approached her, let her handle the situation. If you love and trust her, then you need to allow her to handle the situation. In the case where a partner is having an affair, or has had an affair, you must remember that this is a symptom of a problem in your relationship. The goal is to work with your partner if you are having problems by communicating what your issues are in the relationship and the two of you working on the issues. If this doesn't resolve anything, then I suggest that you get outside help by getting into couples counseling. (See Chapter 10.)

Remember, some people have concerns about going to a therapist and feel that there is a social stigma associated with seeking professional help. Therapy doesn't mean that you or your partner, or both of you, are crazy. It simply means that sometimes we need someone who is outside our situation to help us see things more clearly.

Relationship problems are like getting lost driving to somewhere you've never been or only been once or twice before. Someone gave you directions but you left the second page at home. So you stop and ask directions from someone who knows the area because you do remember the street name and address of where you are going. A good therapist is the person you stop and ask for directions.

How to discuss sexually transmitted diseases

There may be a lower incidence of sexually transmitted diseases in lesbians than in any other population, but that doesn't mean that this should not be discussed, especially if one of you does have a sexually transmitted disease. In most states, you are required by law to tell a potential sexual partner if you have a sexually transmitted disease. Even if no infection occurs and you are using safer sex, you can still be prosecuted. In some states this is considered a felony offense.

It can be very uncomfortable broaching the subject of STDs with someone you are interested in. Gauging the time to do this is the hard part. Obviously, you want to do this prior to being intimate with the other person and not after. This conversation is to protect both you and your potential partner. You need to check with the other person regarding high-risk sexual behaviors she may have had in the past with other people, and you need to share the same information. You'll also need to discuss safer sex practices and her willingness to use them, and also her willingness to get tested for HIV, and hepatitis B if you feel it is necessary. If the test results come back negative on both of you, you can ask your health care professional when it would be OK to have unprotected sex, unless you both have agreed to have an open relationship. Then you get to discuss a whole new topic—how to handle that situation.

It may be uncomfortable to broach the subject with a new partner about STDs, safer sex, and past risky sexual behavior, but the possible end result if you don't could be contracting a fatal or serious illness. Truth be told, there is no good time to bring this up and discuss this topic. The best thing to do is to just jump in and start asking questions after prefacing them with something like, "I'm not sure how to bring this up, but I would like to discuss something important with you to protect us both . . ." If you are not comfortable with this statement, find something that you are comfortable with and use it to open up the discussion. Sometimes it is hard to judge when you should broach the subject, especially since the standard joke about lesbians is "What does a lesbian bring with her on the first date? A U-haul." You are the best judge of when to talk about sexual matters and concerns, as you can sense when the two of you are moving to that place of increased sexual attraction.

Pillow talk

One of the hard things about a new relationship for some is the difficulty in telling your partner what you do and do not want sexually. There may be something that she does in those intimate moments that is really a turn-off for you. If you are uncomfortable with asking your partner to do or say certain things during sex, have a discussion outside the bedroom and at a neutral time. The goal here is to reach the point, if you're not there already, to be able to tell her exactly what you want and how you want it while you are together in bed. And make sure to use basic rules of communication discussed earlier in this chapter.

Let your partner know that this is what you want to talk about, and open the discussion in a calm and clear manner. It may even help you to plan out what you want to cover prior to your talk. Let her know what the issue(s) is(are) and what makes you comfortable, and ask her what she wants. Work on points of compromise as long as you feel that you can compromise over whatever the concern or issue is.

In summary, be open, honest, and compassionate when discussing issues or concerns with your partner and follow the rules contained in this chapter. It won't stop you from arguing, but hopefully it will stop you from fighting, and give you two an opportunity to communicate openly and honestly, and to learn about yourself and each other.

CHAPTER 5

Romance and the art of making lesbian love

The reason I decided to write this chapter is because I've had multitudes of discussions with all kinds of people whose relationships have broken up because of lack or romance, or because they were dissatisfied with their sex lives. Most people who are having relationship troubles stemming from sex seem to truly want to make their partners happy, but are too embarrassed to talk about it to anyone. Many women complain that their partners just don't know what to do, and some of these women have very little knowledge of their own bodies and what it takes to please themselves.

Now, I'm not saying that everyone should go off and masturbate for days on end, but it does help to know yourself. Believe it or not, there are some women who have never masturbated or had an orgasm! I know this for a fact, because I've been with two such women myself.

My first partner had never been with anyone, and she knew nothing about masturbation. We brought each other out at sixteen. My second partner had been married to a man for a while, and then was with a woman for seven years. She'd been with two people for extended periods of time and had no idea about what a clitoris or a G-spot was. She'd never had an orgasm in her entire life! I thought I could certainly remedy that, but for the longest time she would not allow me to give her a clitoral orgasm. She just could not handle the intense feelings of arousal. After a year together, and with her permission, I finally held her down one night, and, believe me, the house practically rocked when she reached orgasm. She was amazed and a whole lot happier being totally satisfied inside and out.

Since this is primarily a coming out book, I thought it would be a good idea to include a few lessons on how to make love to a woman. If you don't know what areola, mons pubis, prepuce, or labia majora mean then you may want to go back and review Chapter 2. I will be using these very important words to explain how to give your partner an orgasm, and it would be good for you to know what I am talking about. There are many ways to make love to a woman, but I just list some basic techniques that I know work for sure. It's up to you to develop your own style, and this explicit step-by-step chapter will help get you started.

Romance, the best way to keep a relationship happy

Romance means different things to different people. Some view being romantic as having dinner ready for their partner the minute she walks in from work, or cleaning the house and washing her clothes. Others view it as candy and kisses, or flowers and dinner dates. The important thing to find in any relationship is what each partner considers romantic, and work towards meeting each other's dreams. This is one way to keep the relationship going for many years, but it's a hard thing to know without asking.

My girlfriend and I just figured this out last weekend, and we've been together over nine years! All this time I was fixing her dinner and doing things that I thought were romantic, only to find out that she was missing romance because her definition was way different than mine. This comes back to the old communication issue that can get neatly swept under the rug because of the business of being alive and making a living. Many of us tend to get caught up in the responsibilities of life, and forget to take time for the fun of it.

Talk to your partner and find out what being romantic means to her. It might come down to just a few words, like "Make wild love to me on a bed of rose petals," or doing something special like cleaning out the cat box and sweeping the floor. Whatever it is, see if you can make her dreams come true. Maybe she will make yours come true too.

Some romantic things to do

Have flowers sent to her at work; send fun cards on all holidays, or when she's feeling blue. These can also be cards you make or even e-mail cards—anything that says you care. Cook her a lovely dinner, using your best plates, even if they are plastic, and maybe use cloth napkins if you have them; turn the lights low and eat by candlelight. If you can't cook, fake it. Buy take-out and put it on plates like you fixed it yourself. Buy snuggly flannel sheets for your bed in the winter, and cool satin ones for the summer. Leave her favorite candy on her pillow, or let her sleep late and serve her breakfast in bed. Tell her how gorgeous she is and how much she means to you whenever you think about it. Give each other romantic body massages, or wonderful foot and hand massages while you are sitting around watching TV.

Encourage and support each other's dreams and goals. Let each other go and do things on your own—not everyone has the same hobbies. Make her something special, or fix something up you find at a garage sale. Have a night each week when you do things together, like have dinner at a nice restaurant or go on a date to see a romantic movie. Play and laugh together. Have deep, long, soul-talks in bed, and make sure to argue somewhere else. Plan short vacation getaways as often as you can afford to. Find fun free things to do, like take the dog for walks at a beautiful place you discover, or drive out in the country to somewhere you've never been. Bring home a funny movie if one of you is sad or depressed. And always, always concentrate on each other's positive qualities.

These are just a few of the things you can do to be romantic. Think of what you would like, and if it seems like your partner would enjoy it, do it for her, but remember we are all different. Make sure to always ask each other what could change to make your relationship better.

First things first

There are as many ways to make love as there are ways to be romantic, so what I'm going to concentrate on are basic techniques that will assure that you can satisfy another woman.

First off, if you are not absolutely positive that either of you has not been exposed to a sexually transmitted disease, make sure you practice safer sex. If you skipped Chapter 3 now would be a good time to read it. I cannot stress how important it is for you to study that chapter. How to have safer sex could save your life, and the descriptions of the diseases and what they can do to you if you catch them should prompt you to never take a risk.

I wrote that chapter so you would be aware of the danger that is out there secretly waiting for the person who thinks "It won't ever happen to me." It scared me when I was doing the research, because when I was young safer sex for lesbians was never discussed. The diseases were out there just the same, and I'm real happy I didn't catch any of them.

I don't want you to catch any of them either. As I said before, I had seventeen friends die of AIDS in one year, and that has had a lasting effect on me. I also have three friends who have hepatitis B, two who have genital herpes, and one who has genital warts. Don't let yourself become a statistic. Read the scary Chapter 3 so that you will never take any chances with your life.

Before foreplay—what to do to get her, and you, in the mood

This is the thing that many people forget, or simply don't understand. Making love with a woman starts in the head and moves south, not the other way around. If you walk up and grab a woman's crotch, she might slap the crap out of you, so don't do that unless you are play fighting and it is a known fact that she is OK with that behavior.

Everyone is different. I had one girlfriend who got aroused by going to the fair, and I knew someone else who would get so turned on in the vegetable section of the grocery store that she would have to leave or face having a spontaneous orgasm next to the cukes. You never know what is going to put someone in the mood, which leads back to communication, but here are a few ideas to begin with:

Take her to a nice restaurant and during dinner rub your foot up her leg under the table cloth. While watching a romantic movie, rub the palm of her hand in the darkness of the theatre, then move up her arm to her breasts. Walk up behind her while she is making lunch and move your breasts across her back while gently kissing her neck. Spontaneous slow dancing in the living room while listening to Melissa Etheridge is always nice. While driving reach over and rub her arm, just barely skimming her breast. Massage her back and then ask to massage her front. Kiss her hands, beginning with the back then going for the palm and her fingers, possibly sucking them into your mouth. While standing, kiss her passionately and gently press your body into hers.

These are just a few of the basic things that can start to turn someone on. Be the detective, find out what it is that she really wants, and then determine if you can do it.

Do not be afraid of being a great lover

When I was first discovering who I was, I read a book about lesbian's fantasies. The woman who wrote it was French and she gave some advice that I never forgot—do not be afraid to do anything to please the woman you love. Now, I don't think she meant you should go beyond your boundaries and hang upside down whipping yourself with a horse crop until you resemble a red-butted baboon, but what I do think she meant was don't limit yourself to what you think you can do. Be open to new experiences, and you will become a great lover.

That brings up another point, which is different in every situation. It is usually better to go slowly and take your time when making love to a woman, but some people don't like it that way. You have to be responsive to what your partner wants in order to fulfill her needs and yours. She may go through times when she wants slow, passionate love, or other times she may ask you to take her on her knees from behind like a dog. You just have to be open enough, and brave enough, to go where she needs you to go and do what she needs you to do. You also need to know your own limitations and be able to openly discuss these when they come up, which goes back to that chapter on communication.

Another important part to making love is cleanliness. Unless your partner likes how you look and smell after mowing your lawn in August, make sure you are as clean as possible. This includes your hair; your hands and fingernails—make sure they are trimmed short, or filed so that there are no rough edges; and most importantly your genitals—no one likes a rolled toilet paper strand as an appetizer, so scrub up! If you tend to have a strong, wild odor about you, then you might want to take a sudsy bath either with or without your partner before making love and maybe even an occasional douche.

So how do I know when she's getting in the mood?

While you are in your before foreplay stage, whatever that might be, there may be signs that show your partner is becoming aroused. She may exhibit any of the following or a combination of them: pupils dilating; dry heat emanating from her chest or upper body; flush on the checks, neck or upper body; chills or goose bumps on any part of her body; harder or accelerated breathing; or small passionate noises or low moans coming from deep in her chest.

You can usually tell when someone is getting turned on by how she is acting. Let the passion build. Don't just take her and throw her down somewhere the minute she shows signs of being aroused, unless she asks you to.

Foreplay, the next step to passion

When your partner starts exhibiting signs of arousal, she may be open to you touching her more intimately. Depending on how she is acting, you might rub her back with the tips of your fingers while lightly kissing her face or neck, or gently massage her arms or legs. Don't just grab her breasts or genitals or force your tongue down her throat. Pay attention to her signals. If they increase, like heavier breathing, more noises, etcetera, then you are still pleasing her.

If you are both inexperienced, she may not know what to do next and she could get scared. Just remain calm, keep doing whatever seems to be working, and remember if she says no, stop right then. Never force anyone to do anything, unless it is part of a sex game that you both have previously agreed upon.

As things heat up, literally, your partner may put your hand where she wants it, or you may have to take the initiative. Depending on if you are standing, sitting, or lying down at this point, ease your hand into her shirt, lightly rubbing her back or stomach, teasing her breasts every now and then. Some women really love their breasts rubbed and some could care less. One of my partners could have an orgasm from that alone. Kiss her lightly as you are massaging near her breasts, then increase your pressure on her mouth, moving down to her neck and shoulders. If she seems receptive to that, then you can either leave her shirt on or take it off, but you need to get where you can put your mouth on her skin.

The move to sexual intimacy

From this point on it is assumed that you are using the safer sex practices listed in Chapter 3. It is up to you to make sure you have the gloves, dental dams, plastic wrap, or whatever you need to protect both yourself and your partner in the place where you plan to make love with her. You might want to have these ready in a drawer next to the bed, under a pillow, or somewhere handy. It's better to plan ahead than to say in a heated moment, "Gotta go get the safer sex stuff. Be right back!" and then run around the house like a horn-dog in heat, rummaging through kitchen drawers for plastic wrap, and digging through your closet for your latex gloves. Nothing chills me more than to have my partner leave the energy that we have created, so be ready for whatever may come up.

At this time you may want to move to where you've stored your safe-sex kit, like a soft couch, piles of blankets in front of a roaring fireplace, or a fluffy bed. Standing up and making love can be hot, but for the first time it might be a little more intimate to be able to relax. Just make sure if you share your house with other people that no one else is going to come bursting through the door. There's nothing worse than having someone walk in while you are half-naked and down on your girlfriend! Believe me, I know.

After moving to the place you've decided on, kiss your partner and either open her shirt or remove it before you lie down beside her. You can do this slowly, rubbing the tips of your fingers up her back as you remove her shirt, or just about rip the shirt off and fall onto the bed with her. It depends on the situation. If your partner seems shy, or inhibited about her body, it may be better to begin making love to her with her clothes partially on so that she doesn't feel totally exposed. Lie down next to her. If you are right-handed you should be on her right side, and if you are left-handed you should be on her left side. This is pretty important, because you definitely want to be using your dominant hand in this situation.

On to the breasts

Tease her a bit more, lightly skimming the areolae of her breasts with the back of your nails. Watch for goose bumps. She may respond by putting her arms around your back and pulling you to her, or she may just lie there and enjoy what you are doing. You can start kissing her neck and shoulders again, gently nipping her with your teeth, while continuing to massage her. Start moving your mouth down towards her breasts. You can use the tip of your tongue, or you can use your lips to nibble her, but be careful of getting too turned on and biting her. This is not Vampire Time at the OK Corral.

You have to remember that while she is getting turned on, so are you, so keep your passion in check enough to be able to judge her responses. Watch how she reacts to what you are doing. If she starts squirming around and makes you stop, then you may be tickling her, and tickling is probably not what you want to do at this very moment.

Gently circle one of her nipples with your mouth. Sometimes it is nice to do the same thing to the other breast with your fingers. See how she is reacting. Is she still breathing hard? Are her nipples responding with hardness? Are her hands clutching at your back or is she kind of just lying there? If she is exhibiting increased passion, then you can probably begin to actually suck her areola into your mouth, gently flicking the nipple with your tongue. You can practice different techniques to see what she responds to most. Some women like their breasts lightly rubbed with the palms of your hands, while others like them yanked and sucked on like a milking machine. Sometimes they will tell you what they like, and sometimes they won't. Just keep checking to make sure she isn't losing interest.

Moving down south

While you are working on her breasts with your mouth and tongue, you can begin to move your hand down her body. Lightly rub her stomach, around the outside of her hips, and the tops of her thighs. Pay close attention to her breathing. If the rate increases, you can gently rub her inner thigh. If she opens her legs, she is nearly ready for you to be truly with her.

She might at this point grab your hand and place it on her mons pubis. Tease her a bit, don't just jump in it. She will love you for it all the more. If her clothes are still partially on, you can probably move back up and unzip her pants. Tease around her bare skin while doing this. Don't rush it. If she has on underwear, gently play under the elastic at the waist. While you are doing all this stuff, you should be also kissing her mouth or breasts. Remember ambidextrous is great but ambiSEXtrous is better!

If you are kissing her mouth, now is a good time to think about what you are going to do to her when you take off her pants. If you are going to go down on her, you might want to practice a bit on her mouth. Gently suck her lips, then run the tip of your tongue over them, and maybe between them and her gums. This usually turns women on big time, because they know that you are going to do the same thing to them somewhere else. Just do this as a tease. Don't lap her face like a basset hound, or make her think that you are cleaning her mouth with your tongue. Basically, don't get too over exuberant, unless she really gets into it. Like I said before, go with what she is showing you. If she seems to not like something you are doing, move on to something else.

Run your fingers over her pants or underwear, teasing over her mons pubis. If she is really responding, you can either have her help you slip her clothes off, or you can sit back up and take them off yourself. It just depends on the moment, but sometimes it is good to have your lover take your clothes off. If she is too shy to remove her clothes at this time, you may have to resort to slipping your hand down her pants and stimulating her. This is a little difficult, but it can be done. Just don't force her to do what she is not ready for.

If she takes her clothes off and then becomes hesitant or shy, then get under the sheets, or cover her with a blanket. Cuddle up to her, and go with what she is showing you. You might have to take a couple of steps back, doing a bit more kissing on her face, neck, hands, etcetera, or she might let you resume where you were. See what she wants, either by her body's response or by what she is saying.

When her passion is back up again, work on her breasts a bit more, kissing her passionately; then glide your hand over her stomach. Enjoy the electricity of her body. You should be able to feel it coming into your palm. Tease around her thighs a bit while kissing her mouth like you want to kiss her down there.

Gently rub over her mons pubis, feel her soft hair. This is where the magic is—when you first touch her there and feel her love being poured out of her body. If you did everything right, and she is way up on the plateau of arousal, she may be wet when you touch her. Some women get soaked and others just lightly mist. You can feel this with latex gloves on, so don't think you will miss the sensation.

Stay with her, look into her eyes, this is the most amazing feeling of being alive. Tell her whatever you need to say from your heart as you move your fingers slowly into her folds. Rub her gently at first, either up and down, or from side to side. Experiment and see what she likes. Keep teasing her with your mouth. Match the slow strokes your hand is making to the slow strokes of your tongue running down her arm and sucking her fingers, or in her mouth or on her breasts. You can make her totally come this way if you aren't quite ready to go down on her.

You should be able to feel her clitoris, although sometimes it will hide. It will feel like a small hard pea within her folds. You can rub it in a circular motion and then slide down into the outside of her opening. This place is extremely sensitive and it usually feels exquisite to be lightly massaged on the outside, just teasing her by letting the tips of one or two of your fingers barely go inside. Continue slowly doing this for a few moments.

She should be quite responsive now, her passion should be way up, and she may be biting your lips, clutching at your back, moaning, talking, or doing a host of other things. Follow her lead. If she opens her legs wide and asks you to go inside, then do it. Some women like to be penetrated, and some do not, some like it first and some like it after they have a clitoral orgasm. Ask her what she needs you to do for her, if you are not sure.

Working towards orgasm

You can either go down on her now, or see if you can stimulate her with your hand enough to have an orgasm. It depends on where you are in your relationship. If you have given yourself orgasms with your fingers, then you kind of know what to do. Start using that technique on her, slow at first, then either increase pressure or stroke her clitoris faster. See how she is responding. She might need you to do it side to side, up and down, or in a circular motion. You can also hold her inner labia and clitoris between both sets of your closed fingers, and gently massage her. You pretty much have to be sitting up between her legs to do this pleasurable little trick. The most important thing about any kind of clitoral stimulation is repetition. If she starts responding by saying "Oh, God, I'm coming," don't change what you are doing. You can do the same thing faster for a more intense orgasm. Just watch for the signs. Some women have a hard time coming from finger stimulation, so ask her what she likes if she is not responding, or have her show you if she is open enough to do so.

If you decide to go down on her, keep rubbing her slowly, teasing her clitoris and softly probing her opening, while you start kissing down her body. Lick her breasts while you are doing this, and keep going down to her stomach. Kiss around her pubic hair. If she is reacting in a positive way, meaning her legs are open and she is not pulling you back up to her face, keep going down.

Gently spread her legs and lower yourself between them. You can kiss her thighs, teasing your face over her pubic hair, which should be covered with dental dam or plastic wrap. Using your fingers on one or both of your hands, spread her outer labia. You can start moving your tongue up through her crevices, gently flicking her clitoris, and then back down again until you reach her entrance. Do this for a little while, keeping the pace slow. Her hips may be moving with your rhythm, her hands may be tangled in your hair, and she should be pretty much in ecstasy.

As her reactions increase, you can either quicken your strokes and see if she comes, or tease her a bit more. She will let you know if she is coming. Either she will start saying she is, or her body will tighten up and then begin to shudder, or she might thrust against your face in time with her contractions. If she doesn't seem to be able to get over that edge, you can use the fingers on both your hands to gently pull both sides of her labia minora up and apart. This will move the skin of the prepuce off the clitoris. Take the tip of your tongue and in a circular motion move it around her clitoris. Do this in a rhythmic way and make sure you keep contact with her clitoris. You can feel it on your tongue. She may come like this or tell you to do it faster. If she doesn't respond you can either carefully suck her clitoris into your mouth, and start rotating your head while swirling the point of your tongue over it, or you can keep lapping her and insert your fingers into her, either hitting her G-spot (Grafenberg) or gently probing her until she comes. If you do the clitoris trick, be careful not to suck too hard. She will either absolutely love this, or she may not like it. It depends on how sensitive her clitoris is.

The next step to total fulfillment

After she has come from her clitoris, you can either wait a few moments and start all over again, or you may want to move up her body and lay on top of her. Don't jump up and leave the bed! She may get a chill and will need you to snuggle with her. While you are moving up, you could slide your fingers inside. Her body should be totally ready for this as long as her mind goes along.

Some women see this as too much like being with a man; others absolutely love it. If your lover feels it is too much like being with a man, you might try lying beside her and entering her that way. To me, there is no feeling in the world as amazing as being inside the woman you love, so hopefully she will be receptive to it.

You can move your hand in and out or in a slow rotation. You can also turn your hand so that the palm is towards whatever she is lying on and gently thrust downward. A lot of women like this because it stimulates the rectum without having to go directly inside of it. As her passion responds to what you are doing, you should start increasing your rhythm. She should be moving with you at this point. As you come to a crescendo, you can curve your fingers up, towards her stomach if she is on her back, and hit her G-spot. The texture will usually feel different than the vaginal wall, and she will go absolutely wild when you hit it. You can either keep thrusting with your fingers curved up, or you can stop thrusting and just move your curved fingers faster, hitting her spot until she has an amazing orgasm. She may or may not ejaculate at this point. If she does, it is totally normal, so don't freak out. It will smell a little stronger than her regular scent and the consistency will be like water, but it is not usually urine.

Most women are unaware that they have this capability, so your partner may be embarrassed if this happens, but assure her that this is normal. If a woman is so turned on that she ejaculates, it is the biggest compliment you could ever get as a lover. It puts you in the realm of electrical equipment, like vibrators, so be proud of yourself and your lover. Just get a towel and use safer sex.

Most women are very capable of having multiple orgasms,

so making love can go on for hours, or until one of you gets too tired to move. On the other hand, if you or your lover has problems achieving orgasm, make sure to read the rest of this chapter. There is more than one way to skin the kitty, as they say.

Some other techniques and positions

In lesbian lovemaking just about anything you can think of can be done, if both partners are willing and able. Using lots of positions and making love in different places are two ways to keep your relationship young at heart. Since I am not the Kama Sutra Goddess, I will just list a few of the more basic ones here. The rest is up to you. Be as wild and brave as possible and you will become a great lover.

Side-to-side

This position is good, especially if you need to be stealthy for some reason—like your lover's straight sister is sound asleep in the same room, also known as being young and kind of dumb, or some other unusual circumstance.

The two facing partners lie on their sides, stimulating each other with only their hands. This can be done by taking turns or in unison. If you need to be really quiet, then it should probably be one at a time. Use good sense and don't get caught in a compromising position.

Standing up

This arrangement can be very wild so it's good to be against a wall for stability. You can either be face-to-face with your partner while your hands are doing the work, or you can be down on your knees with your mouth and fingers having a little "crotchety" party. If you are doing the latter, be warned. Safer sex is pretty hard in this position, unless your partner has on adult-sized plastic training pants.

Straddling

This position is when one partner is lying on her back, and the other is straddling her lap or stomach. The person lying down can be stimulating her partner either clitorally or vaginally. The partner on top can also move her body against her lover, known as tribadism or grinding, which will stimulate her clitoris, or move her body with her lover's fingers or a dildo inside of her.

Sitting up

This is a highly erotic position that can be done in a roomy chair, on a couch, on the floor, or in the bed. It is kind of nice if you've just given your partner an oral orgasm, to sit up and pull her into your lap. You can put one arm around her back for support, have your fingers deep inside of her, curved towards her stomach and hitting her G-spot, and be kissing her passionately all at the same time. She can also choose to move her body on your fingers, hitting all the right spots and giving your tired arm muscles a rest.

Sitting up—on her face

Speaking of erotic, if your knees and thighs can handle this position, you can come like a wild coconut-humpin' monkey! You can do this straddling her head frontwards or backwards. She can put her fingers in you, and at the same time you can move your body on her mouth for the ultimate clitoral orgasm. A little warning though. Safe sex in this position is difficult, but it can be done. Just be careful not to smoother your partner with the latex or plastic barrier. Another thing is to make sure your partner knows what you mean when you ask her to sit on your face. I heard one story of a poor woman who was almost suffocated when her inexperienced lover plopped down on her face like she was sitting on a fluffy love seat.

The ol' 69

Lots of people joke around about doing 69, but few lesbians can really do it right. If you don't know what it is, just look at the number—it's both partners performing oral action at the same time. Now you can do this on your sides, or one on top of the other, but it is not the easiest position in the world. I think it's harder for most of us because our vaginas are a little difficult to get to. Unless you happen to be with Janice the Giraffe-Necked Woman, I would say leave 69 to the people who are best at it, or use it for some fun foreplay.

From behind

This position can be done either with one partner on her knees and the other one behind her, or one partner lying on her side or stomach with the other stimulating her from behind. Depending on the circumstances, this position can either be totally erotic, or totally threatening. I was pretty much raped by a woman this way one time, and it freaked me out because I had no way to get out from under her weight. She did not pay attention to the fact that I was really having a problem, and I never trusted her intimately again.

If you want to try making love from behind, make sure to discuss it, or if it is something that naturally happens one time when you are together, just make sure that your partner is OK with this kind of vulnerability.

Anal sex

Some people love anal sex and others can't stand it. I have one bisexual woman friend who would rather have anal sex than vaginal intercourse. It just depends on the person. This is another communication issue. Just don't go cramming something in your partner's rectum unless you know for sure this is what she wants.

If you decide you'd like to try anal sex, it's best to start out small, say with one well-lubricated finger. Finger cots are great for anal sex and some sort of protection should always be used. As with vaginal sex, start out slowly and see how your lover responds. She might like you to swirl your finger in a circular motion on the outside and then slowly move in, or she might like a bit of pumping action. If you are entering her from behind, you can have one finger in her anus and the thumb of your other hand in her vagina with your index finger stimulating her clitoris. Talk about being filled up! Just remember, never use toys or fingers in the anus and then in the vagina. This is a sure-fire way of giving your partner the biggest, nastiest infection of her life, so always use fresh condoms or wash your toys with soap and hot water between activities. Make sure if they are battery operated toys that you do not get water inside the battery compartment. The contacts will rust and you will have a vibrator that doesn't vibrate. Also, do not insert small objects into the anus, because they have a way of disappearing. You sure don't want to spend the night in the emergency room explaining how that fem-looking size 5 ring got lodged way up inside your butt.

The illusive and unusual scissors

Well, I can't say much about this position, especially since I've never successfully done it. The two partners are supposed to be able to straddle each other and mutually rub their vulvas together, stimulating each other to a wonderful mutual clitoral orgasm. Kind of like two Vs meeting in the middle at their crotches. All I can say is good luck and more power to you if you can get off doing this. I ended up with a bruise the size of a half dollar from my partner's pubic bone slamming into mine, and this is not anything I'd want to do again. I do know some women who love this position, but if you decide to try it, do so with caution.

Butt to butt

This unusual position works best when using a double-headed dildo. Both partners are on their knees, butt to butt, with the dildo inside both of them. If done gently, this can be pretty erotic, but be warned. If one partner gets a little to energetic, her movement can cause the other side of the dildo to go too deep into her partner, causing pain and possible injury. I knew of two women who were using a double-header and got a little too energetic. The dildo slipped and one of the women ended up having her perineum torn apart. She had to go to the emergency room and have it stitched up, a rather embarrassing and painful situation. Use all vibrators and toys cautiously as described in the next section.

Adult toys—let's take the pleasure a step further

Some women like toys and others are too proud to admit that they might. I feel that

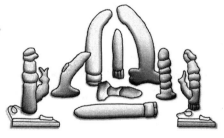

Various dildos and battery operated toys

anything which enhances your time together, or alone, is perfectly OK. Besides, it can be really nice after a hard-core love-making session to get out the ol' vibrator and watch your lover have five more orgasms before she falls deeply asleep in your arms.

Sometimes, women find it hard to have an orgasm from hand or mouth stimulation and need a vibrator. If this is true for you or your partner, don't be embarrassed about it. Just be honest so that no one feels they are not a good enough lover to make the other person come. Have regular foreplay, then let the vibrator become an extension of yourself.

What's the best kind of vibrator?

Depending on where and what you want to stimulate, there are many types and styles of vibrators to choose from. There are some that use electricity and others that

The Jett

use batteries; some look like penises, bananas, and even cats, and some are smooth and look like little rockets. There are some that are curved to hit the G-spot, and there are some like little butterflies that you can wear inside your clothes. Silicone is always the best material for toys. Because it is nonporous, it doesn't harbor bacteria and can be easily cleaned with antibacterial soap and hot water.

You can buy vibrators and dildos at some home lingerie parties, or your local adult store. If you can't imagine walking into a sex store, you can buy adult toys online or by mail order (see the index for a list of suppliers.) If you want to know what it is like to go into some of these sex stores, read my novel, *Above Faith, Beyond Fear* for a fictionalized account of one of my own visits.

The best toy I've found for multiple clitoral orgasms is the regular handheld massager that you can buy at almost any drug store. I have one I call "The Jett," and I swear it could about make a dead person come. These handheld massagers usually have several attachments, which you can experiment with. The bell-shaped one, shown in the illustration, seems to work the best for me. You can either place it on the top or either side of your prepuce, because it is too strong to put directly on the clitoris.

The most important thing when using one of these vibrators is that you should be as dry as possible in your outer vulva area. If the revolutions per minute are fast enough, it can burn you, so use a dry towel and wipe yourself off before placing the vibrator near your delicate parts. If it is too strong use some soft cloth between you and the vibrator. Also, these things can be powerful enough to cause a woman to ejaculate. Make sure not to do this on the vibrator! Remember, this is an electrical appliance. It can short-out or shock you if you soak it down, so don't be using it in the tub either. I sure don't want to read about your untimely, orgasmic death on the front page of some rag magazine at the local supermarket. So use good sense and put a towel between you and the vibrator if you think you might rain all over the place. If you are using the vibrator on your partner, also have plastic wrap along with the towel, to keep it safe for both of you.

Another thing you can do with a handheld massager is use it with a hollow dildo. Find the attachment that best fits inside of the dildo and turn it on while it's inside of you or your partner. This can produce a very intense orgasm, especially if you have it angled up towards the G-spot, or down towards the rectum, which also stimulates the clitoris. If you use a handheld vibrator in this way, lubrication is a must, along with a condom for switching out if with a partner. The dildo will take most of the rpm, so it should not burn anyone who is using it. Just make sure to protect the vibrator from getting wet. You can also use a dildo or internal vibrator while performing oral sex for a double orgasm—whatever you and your partner are in the mood for.

Does wanting to use a dildo mean I might be a closet straight?

No, it doesn't. What it does mean is that you might need more to fill you than a few fingers. Remember, we are lesbians living in physical bodies that have their own needs. Just because you would like something bigger inside of you, does not mean anything about being straight. It just means you like to feel filled up.

Now some women like this all the time, and some never want anything, like fingers or dildos, inside of them. That's perfectly OK too. You have to decide if it is something you can live without doing. If you have the constant urge to be inside the woman you love, or to perform any other kind of sexual activity, and she will not allow you to do what you yearn to do, it can have dire consequences on your relationship.

To be a great lover, you have to be able to go with what your partner needs. If she begs you to strap one on and do her from behind, then it is up to you to decide if you can or not. This comes back to communication. Discuss new things you want to do before you are at that point in the heat of passion. Nothing can be more disappointing than fantasizing all day about some radical new position or toy, only to have your lover say, "No way!"

If you find that you or your partner are having chronic sexual difficulties, you might want to read the section at the end of this chapter concerning the signs of and how to handle childhood sexual abuse issues.

Shower heads

Another fun way to have clitoral orgasms, either by yourself or with a partner, is with a pulsating shower massage. Make sure the water is not too hot, and always have the stream of water pointing down across your clitoris and away from your vaginal opening. Some of these shower massagers are very powerful, so NEVER point the stream up into your vagina. You could get a nasty infection or even worse an injury, so use caution when using water appliances.

Other ways of being sexual

Trisexuals, the three-way affair

Threesomes, hmmm, what can I say? Have I ever done it? Yes. Would I do it again? No. Why? It was just too weird the next morning, and when it got out to the small Southern lesbian community I was a part of at that time, my lover and I were completely shunned.

Now I'm sure times have changed since the early eighties, but I'm not sure how much. I will say this, if you are in the beginning of a relationship, I would not suggest having a threesome. It just puts too much stress on a growing partnership. If you are out being wild and sowing your oats, using safer sex all the time, then maybe you can handle it. It just depends on who you are and what you want.

As with most other forms of human sexuality, I have nothing against threesomes. The upside was it was erotic, and it was fun. The downside was it tore my relationship of seven years apart and ruined a nice friendship I had with the woman who was our third party.

It also surprised me how other lesbians reacted when they found out. I was picked up and groped by a butch weight-lifter at a Metropolitan Community Church volleyball game, publicly humiliated at an art show where I was exhibiting, and totally ostracized from a community who expects everyone else not to ostracize them. It was a hard lesson I learned in my early twenties and one I don't wish to repeat. If you decide to have a threesome, just be forewarned. At least in my case, the pain totally outweighed the pleasure.

Fetishes

A fetish is usually something that causes sexual arousal. It may be anything from wearing spike-heeled boots or leather or rubber clothing, to looking at certain body parts or even cucumbers sold at your local market. Sometimes fetishists require that their object be present during sex to achieve an orgasm, or they may have to fantasize about it in order to heighten their arousal to bring on an orgasm. Having a fetish is not bad, unless it is something that freaks out your partner. Again, communication is the issue here. If you have a fetish that is too bizarre for words, you may want to just visualize it instead of making it a part of your sex play with someone else.

Sadism and masochism (S&M)

Sadism is defined as an intentional infliction of pain or humiliation which brings on arousal and sexual excitement. Masochism means getting sexually aroused from being hurt or humiliated. I guess you can see what a perfect fit these two types of people are and why their relationship is called S&M.

The word sadism comes from the French author, Marquis DeSade, who wrote about using cruelty for sexual gratification in the late 1700s. The word "masochism" was named after Leopold Baron Von Sacher-Masoch. He wrote *Venus in Furs* in 1888, which was all about the pleasures of pain.

I have known some lesbians who are into mild forms of S&M, that included spankings, master-slave relationships, and some forms of bondage. As with everything else in this book, I believe that whatever two consenting adults do in private is certainly none of my business. If you love being turned over your partner's knee and smacked on your bare butt, more power to you.

On the other hand, I have known lesbians who took

S&M to extremes and actually brutalized their lovers until they could no longer function as regular human beings. These women became like chained dogs, totally dependent on their "master" or "mistress." I'm not so sure how good it is to be tied up in a tub of freezing water and have a live 8-foot boa constrictor thrown on you, or spend hours chained to a bed with a spiked dog collar choking you if you move.

I do believe some of the more intense forms of cruelty stem directly from the reenactment of childhood abuse. Whether this is on a conscious or subconscious level, it really doesn't matter. What does matter is the fact that a relationship like this usually ends in someone getting hurt or even killed. If the abused person escapes, it can end in years of therapy or finding another person who will fill her needs to be punished.

Just like everything in life, a little can be great, but a lot can be detrimental to your mental or physical health. If you find that you are having fantasies of physically maiming someone for sexual pleasure, it might stem from something that happened to you when you were a child. The same goes for if you have constant fantasies of being terribly hurt to achieve an orgasm. In either case, you might want to read the next section or seek professional help.

Childhood abuse: sexual, physical, and emotional

It is a known fact that at least one in four females and one in six males are subjected to some kind of childhood sexual abuse. Since I am a member of the one in four females group, I take ending child abuse personally. Abuse was a large part of my daily life growing up, and it took me years to recover as an adult. I still have problems to this day, and believe me I've been through lots of therapy and read many self-help books.

I believe child abuse is the number one reason we have so much crime in today's world. It is a horrible heritage that has been passed down for generations, and it is up to us to stop it.

Now some people will balk at what I'm about to write, but I totally believe my soul chose to be born into child abuse so that I could do something about it when I grew up. All of my novels have characters who are survivors and have flourished as adults, just like I have. These books are written for the one out of four of us who need a positive role model, someone who made it through the hell of her past

I know this is a hard subject to think about; it's hard for me to admit that it happened to me, but if we don't think about it and learn what the signs are, then nothing will change. Look around you. One in four of your female friends has experienced some sort of abuse. That's just too much! We don't talk about it. We sweep it under some moldy rug somewhere, where it grows into something that can no longer be hidden. When the flashbacks and fear of abandonment start, they can ruin your relationship with the person you love most. Listen to what I am saying here, because my first two serious relationships ended because I was too emotionally sick to know I needed help.

What is considered sexual abuse?

Sexual abuse takes many forms. These are some of the more common: inappropriate touching or kissing of your genitals; being fondled, kissed, or held on the lap of someone with an erection; raped rectally or vaginally; shown sexual magazines or movies; any kind of ritualized S&M whether sexual or not; being ridiculed concerning the development of your body; being talked to in a sexually inappropriate way; or being forced to be a child prostitute or pose for pornographic movies or photos.

Sometimes women remember what happened and sometimes they don't. If you or your lover is exhibiting some of the following symptoms, there may be a reason to investigate your past a little deeper, with either a qualified therapist or counselor.

Symptoms of childhood sexual abuse

There are many symptoms of sexual abuse including the following: the need to control everything about sex; problems being close in nonsexual ways; confusing sex with affection; being the absolute best in everything sexual (that's why I could write this chapter); experiencing flashbacks of abuse when making love; getting aroused by thinking about sexual abuse; having a hard time trusting anyone; not staying emotionally with your partner when making love, meaning you are thinking of anything else but what is going on; having fear of having children or being overprotective of children; experiencing recurring thoughts that you don't deserve to be with anyone; suffering from abandonment issues—always fearing someone will leave you; feeling you are different from others; having intense fear or terror when you think about being intimate; hating yourself or feeling the need to kill yourself; being scared of success or failure; experiencing frequent nightmares; being fearful of violence or of being violent or abusive to someone else; having any kind of eating disorder; avoiding sex altogether; thinking that sex is disgusting or dirty; having the inability to set limits, whether sexual or not; feeling taken advantage of in all of your relationships; or dating someone who is like your abuser either physically or emotionally.

These are just some of the symptoms of childhood sexual

abuse. During my life I have had thirteen of these symptoms, although I only have a couple of them occasionally now. One thing I do know is if I can heal, so can you.

If you had any kind of abuse as a little girl, it affected you whether you realize it or not. I did not know how much it hurt me until I was in my twenties. I would be with my partner, and just about to have an orgasm, when I would have a total flashback of my uncle going down on me at four years old. Talk about an orgasm leaving in a hurry. That's what it felt like. One second it was there, the next it dissolved into the past, leaving me with chronic fear that was coiled in my stomach—which eventually turned into an ulcer.

This is the type of thing that sneaks up on you when you least expect it. This is the gift of child abuse, but you can choose to do something about it. You will always have those memories but they don't have to ruin your whole life. Choose to be healthy. Choose to break the pattern of mental illness. Choose your life. Success is the best revenge against something so horrible. Use your gifts. Turn your pain around and do something for yourself and the world.

If you don't feel like you can discuss what happened to you with a therapist, then go get *The Courage to Heal* book and workbook. It helped me more than all of my years of therapy combined. It made me realize how much the abuse affected the life I am living now, and it helped me to change the patterns that resulted in all of my failed intimate relationships. The book was coauthored by a lesbian, so it is totally friendly for anyone who wants to take back the control in her life from her abuser.

If you are the type of person who needs to understand why child abuse happens, the best book I ever read on the subject was *Bradshaw on the Family* by John Bradshaw. This book discusses how family patterns are passed down from one generation to the next. It made it very clear for me to see how my childhood was destroying my adult life, and it gave me ways to stop the patterns that were ingrained in me.

If you were physically, mentally, or sexually abused as a child, these patterns can sneak up on you and surface as abuse in your adult relationships. Since this is more common in lesbian relationships than most of us would like to admit, I've included the following section to illustrate the forms of abuse some of us may be living in.

Domestic Partner Abuse

Abuse in a lesbian relationship can be defined as any behavior your partner uses to control you, which causes physical, sexual and/or psychological damage, or causes you to live in fear. The following are some types of partner abuse:

Emotional Abuse

This is a painful kind of abuse where your partner puts you down, calls you names, and generally makes you feel bad about yourself to your face or in front of other people. She may play mind games to make you think it is your problem or tell you that you are crazy or stupid. She may encourage self-hatred about being lesbian or force you to be closeted. She may use blackmail to control you, treat you like a servant, or threaten murder or suicide so that you are too afraid for your own life, or hers, to make a change.

Isolation

When an abuser uses isolation, she is controlling what you do, such as who you see and talk to, or where you go. She may not allow you to be involved in lesbian community, and she may sabotage any new friendships that you try to form outside of the relationship. She may maintain a heterosexual pretense in order to keep you isolated. The abusive partner may use jealousy to justify her actions.

Intimidation and Threats

This kind of abuse usually begins at home, but as your abuser gains confidence of her control of you she may do some of the following in public situations: using looks, actions, or gestures to make you afraid; driving unsafely when you are in the car to scare you; destroying your general possessions or cherished items; abusing pets or children; buying weapons and showing them to you; or threatening to "out you" at work or to your friends or family.

Physical Abuse

This abuse usually happens in the privacy of your home and can include pushing, biting, hitting, punching, using a weapon, or forcing you to participate in sex. If you try to flee, your abuser may attempt to confine you physically. If you are injured, your abuser may prevent you from going to a doctor, or she may control your food or medication. If you are severely injured, your abuser may take you to a hospital, but threaten you with further physical abuse if you do not lie about what happened. She may say she is directly related to you, and accompany you to the examining room. She may speak for you and not allow you to be alone with a health-care practitioner.

Sexual Abuse

Sexual abuse can take many forms, but generally it is defined as any sexual activity that is unwanted or coerced. Also included are non-disclosure of STD/HIV status; sexual name calling; accusations of you wanting to have or having sex with other women or friends; or your abuser may threaten to have sex with others or force you to become pregnant or to terminate an existing pregnancy.

Using Children

If you have children from a previous relationship, your abuser may use them to keep you in control. Some ways of doing this are: threatening to expose your relationship so that your children are taken away; telling your children bad things about you; using visitation of the other parent to harass you; making sarcastic remarks about your parenting abilities; or refusing to allow you to see your children if you don't have full custody.

Economic Abuse

When an abuser controls you economically she may prevent you from getting or keeping a job outside the home, and demand that you ask for money or an allowance from her. If you are allowed to work, she may take any money you make. She may not allow you to participate in financial decision-making, or may deny your rights to any assets within the partnership. She may threaten to "out you" at work so that you lose your job and are financially dependent upon her.

Patterns of abuse and abuser justification

Abuse and abusers follow a pattern of gradual escalation. The abuse usually starts out slowly with harsh criticisms, then apologies. At first the incidents happen without any regular frequency. Then they escalate. It doesn't matter which form of abuse is employed. Eventually it escalates until the abuse is the norm and those periods of getting along are few and far between. Most people react by objecting to abuse, and their partner may verbally and/or physically respond.

When an abuser reaches a point that she knows you have been pushed too far, or that she has frightened herself by the violence she has perpetrated, her reaction may be to say that she didn't mean to be abusive. She may make light of the abuse and blame you for her behavior. When asked about the abuse, she may say that it didn't happen, or that you are the one who is abusive. She may blame stress as a problem or say she had a traumatic childhood. She may use drinking or drug abuse as an excuse, or say that society oppresses her as a lesbian. She may say she can't control her anger, or that she can't express her feelings appropriately.

Since abuse is usually something that builds slowly, the abused begins to make excuses for the abuser and take blame herself. She may also be seduced by how romantic or attentive her partner becomes and want with all her heart to believe that this is the reality of the relationship, that this is how her partner really is. The reality is that the longer the process is allowed to continue, the norm becomes abuse and the exceptions are the good times.

No matter what the excuse is, abuse is wrong. All of us experience life's problems, but we don't go around beating or belittling everyone else in order to cope. Abusive lesbians are using control to get their own way and to keep their partners under their thumbs. They CAN control their abuse, but choose to control another person instead.

How you may feel:

If you are in an abusive relationship, you may be ashamed to tell anyone. This is especially bad if your friends or family do not know you are lesbian, which can lead to feelings of depression, humiliation, and increased isolation. Many abused women blame themselves, thinking that they have failed the relationship in some way, such as not being a good enough lover, partner, or parent. They may feel guilty or scared to leave their partner. Many hold on to the hope that their partner will change. This is often reinforced with apologies after the abuse has taken place like "I swear it will never happen again," or "I promise it won't—please don't leave me." When the abuse happens again, it sets up a pattern where the abuser knows she has gotten away with it one time, so she thinks she can do it over and over again.

So why do lesbians remain in abusive relationships? Some believe they can't leave because they are not financially secure. Others think that the abuse wouldn't be happening if they didn't deserve it. In most cases, this last belief comes directly from childhood abuse.

When we were growing up, many of us were taught that adults are always right. "I brought you into this world, and I can take you out" was a very common statement in my childhood home. To many kids this translates to "If Mom and Dad are beating me and threatening my life, then something must be wrong with me," or "I must have done something wrong." This can set up a pattern in your adult years where you view, or you subconsciously view, anyone who abuses you as acting in a correct way. It can lead you to believe that you are responsible for your partner's violence, but this is simply not true.

No matter what happened when you were little, abuse in any form is WRONG. It is up to you to change the way you think of it. Now whether this means finding a good therapist and working on it, or getting the *The Courage to Heal Workbook, For Women and Men Survivors of Child Sexual Abuse*, it is up to you to do something to make a change.

Things you can do:

The most important thing you can do is pay attention to how you feel. If you are in a new relationship and you find a pattern of abuse developing, talk to staff at a spouse abuse shelter, a counselor, or a friend. You can also do research at the library or on the Internet to verify your feelings. Check the index for some some websites where you can find support and help.

If you want to work on the relationship, you and your partner both need to get into some kind of therapy or couples counseling. If you feel safe, you can discuss this with her. Abuse is a behavior that can be hard to change, but abusers can change if they realize how detrimental it is not only to their partner but to themselves as well.

There should always be a safe place for you to go if the abuser reverts back to her old ways. You may have to rely on friends or family. Have your friends or family be present if you need to see your abuser for any reason. Have a code word that you can use to notify them if she suddenly shows up, or that things are not so good and you need help. Change your phone number and door locks and have an answering machine to screen all of your calls.

If your relationship has developed into an abusive one and you want to get out of it permanently, you may no longer have any friends or family contacts. It may also be that if you do have friends or family still in your life, your abuser may have threatened their safety to control you.

If things get really bad—physical assault, sexual assault, threats, or stalking—you may have to talk to the police about legal options such as a restraining order or criminal charges. Some states charge for a restraining order, but some will waive the cost if you can't afford to pay.

Make a detailed plan to escape. Leave when your abuser is not at home and take clothing and personal items you may need. If you have family or friends and they haven't been threatened, you may be able to use them for a safe house. If you don't feel it is safe to go to your family or friends, call your local spouse abuse shelter and ask for help and a place to stay. Most shelters have safe houses. Some admit people who have only experienced physical abuse and some will take you in if you have experienced verbal abuse. Once at the shelter you will be safe, and the staff there can help with counseling, community resources, legal advice, and assistance in filing a restraining order. Your life is up to you. Either be a victim and let your abuser win, or use your gifts and be the success you are meant to be. You have to be strong enough to release the past, and brave enough to change the pattern that was ingrained in you from your youth. Only we can stop the abuse and become the incredible people we are meant to be. I'm sitting at my keyboard typing the truth of my life, in hopes that maybe what happened to me can help you, or someone you know, to make a move towards healing. Take back your power now, and turn it into something beautiful.

CHAPTER 6

Dealing with the outside world

MCs and closet cases

Some people would rather keep a picture of us being "just good friends," in their minds than to imagine two women going at it. Maybe it would turn them on too much, or maybe they would be jealous because of the multiple orgasms that lesbians are capable of, or maybe they don't want to face something within themselves. Whatever the reason, most straight people I know are fine with the fact that I am lesbian, as long as I don't talk about it too much. I have also found that many of the people who are homophobic, or disturbed by who I am, are unsure of their own sexuality. My girlfriend and I term some of these people "MCs" (for "missed their calling"). And then there are the "closet cases," a breed all their own.

You can spot MCs everywhere you go, especially when they are a "straight" couple. The man will seem totally gay and the woman will seem lesbian, and the couple will be quite obvious to anyone who has an ounce of Gaydar. Sometimes they will not have a clue that they have missed their calling, and can live their whole lives together in a loving friendship. Some are not satisfied with their lives, but never quite know why.

Different from the MCs are the "closet cases." Closet cases know in their hearts that they are lesbian or bisexual, but will not admit it to themselves or others. They didn't miss their calling, they simply refuse to accept it. Some live in conventional "straight" relationships, but have secret same-sex lovers on the side. Other times they force themselves to be straight or celibate, and subsequently they are not happy. These are the people to watch out for. They are the ones who will seduce you into affairs, then call you sick; glare at you in public situations and whisper about you behind your back; and some may even tell your boss and coworkers that you are queer. The ones I've been in contact with always seem to want to make my life as miserable as possible. I believe they do this on a subconscious level in order to validate their belief that being gay is a horrible existence. It seems they hate their own gayness so much that they project their hatred away from themselves and onto some other person.

The funny thing about MCs and closet cases is this: if being a homo is a biological thing, which most scientists are saying it is, then wouldn't people who are gay but are "choosing" to be straight have more of a chance of producing queer kids? And if this is true, then all the televangelists who are telling everyone that they can "choose to be straight" are really helping to bring more homos into the world. Hmmm, now isn't that something to ponder? Instead of us luring straight god-fearin' people into our lifestyle, they are actually helping us to be born! Think about this as we touch on the next section.

The radical Christian Reich-I mean right!

Since I am not a member of the radical Christian right, I cannot really tell you what they are planning or thinking. I will say this, I believe Jesus was a real human being who graced this earth with his presence long ago. He had a lot of wonderful things to say and teachings that are still good to this day. He hung out with prostitutes and thieves, and he respected people for who they were, no matter what. As far as the translated text goes, he never said a word about homosexuality. He loved unconditionally and he did not judge his fellow human beings.

So why do so many of his followers do what he said was wrong? Who gave them the "right" to be hurtful and judgmental? To spurn members of their church if they come out? To harass them until they leave their hometowns? To tie us to fences and leave us to die? To beat us to death in cold alleys? Just who is the culprit here?

When asked these questions, many of the radical Christian right will immediately claim their total obedience of God's word, which to them means the whole Bible. Well, if they are truly into the Bible and really believe that it is the end-all truth, then why aren't these people selling their children into slavery, as sanctioned in Exodus 21:7, or purchasing their own slaves, as stated in Lev. 25:44? Why aren't they putting people to death who work on Sunday, as stated in Exodus 35:2, or stoning people who curse too much as instructed in Lev. 24:10-16? Why are many of them still eating shellfish, a big no-no according to Lev. 11:10; cutting the hair around their temples, forbidden by Lev. 19:27; and wearing garments made of two different kinds of thread? Can they really be that selective about what they believe? Or was the Bible written so they could just a pick and choose their prejudice?

Now I'm not accusing the radical Christian right of going out and doing all the dirty deeds that have happened to gay people. I'm sure just like any group, there are good people involved who are not aware of how deep the hatred goes, or how it can affect someone's life. What I am saying is that the negative influence of some can be felt throughout the whole country, and it does affect how many people think.

What is the deal with the "Gay Agenda?"

The Gay Agenda is a 23-minute videotape that was released in 1992 by Springs of Life Ministries. Located outside Los Angeles, California, Springs of Life Ministries even had the infamous Jim Bakker preaching there in 1987. The Gay Agenda video was released during the time that people in Colorado and Oregon were working for the antigay rights campaign. It was handed out free to people in grocery store parking lots, door to door, and in many churches. Excerpts were aired on Pat Robertson's 700 Club, and in some areas the entire tape was shown on cable TV. It was sent to top officers in the military and was used as an antigay training film in some circumstances. All 594 members of Congress received one. Basically, it was sent to areas that were considering equal rights for gays.

I have never seen this film myself, but I've been told by people who have that it shows a lot of different behaviors that both heterosexuals and homosexuals are into, like transvestism, S&M, 1-900 phone sex lines, costume parades, nudity, and just plain-out being wild and outrageous. It does this with the message that there is a radical gay plot to undermine straight people and change them into what they fear most. In 1993 the Springs of Life Ministries also produced a video entitled The Gay Agenda in Public Education, which is said to expose a radical homosexual plot to weaken young people in schools, making it easier for us to convert them.

These videos remind me of Nazi Germany and the propaganda films that were shown against Jewish people, and look how that turned out. All I can say is that I've been a card-totin' lez most of my life, and I have yet to attend a meeting where gay people are conspiring to take over the world or infiltrate schools. Shoot, we can't even agree on what kind of food to bring to a potluck dinner, much less overthrow the government or the religious foundation of a free nation.

Now I'm not claiming that all gay people are lily white innocents who never do anything wrong. There is good and bad in every group, but to show only the bad is not fair to anyone.

What if I went around and taped married men making passes at younger women, drinking like pigs, having lap dances at strip clubs, beating and raping their wives, fighting drunkenly in the street, and just plain acting lewd? What if I edited in some phone sex from a straight 1-900 line, and then added film of a father molesting his daughter? What if I overlaid a track of a straight mom verbally and physically abusing her kids in the privacy of her home, and then made commentary that heterosexuals are trying to infiltrate our culture and make us abusive, weirdo, alcoholics, like they are? Would that video be a fair portrayal of what it is to be straight? Of course not!

So who really is the radical group here? How can anyone turn anyone into anything? I mean most of us were raised in a full-fledged heterosexual world with non-stop advertising of hetero sex, hetero relationships, male dominance, violence, and insanity. Flip through the TV channels or any magazine and check out the advertisements. How many women are shown doing anything but selling something at any given moment and usually using straight sexuality to do it. With all this straight programming, why aren't we hetero? Could it be that no one can make anyone anything? But according to the Gay Agenda videos, we are scheming and concocting plans to turn true-blooded heterosexuals into flaming queers and diesel dykes! How can this happen if the true-blooded heterosexual doesn't want to do it? Maybe the religious right thinks we are using some of the brainwashing techniques used in some of the "Going Straight" programs. If so, I sure want nothing to do with it.

As long as child or animal abuse is not involved, I don't care what anyone does. If you are happy, then I am happy for you. I raised a daughter in a lesbian relationship for nine years, and she sure didn't turn out gay. I was honest with her about how hard it can be to be different in this world, but I never purposely influenced her either way. How could I?

From the day we are born, most of us are pushed nonstop to be straight, and when it comes down to it we just are what we are. It's not a new thing, and no matter what anyone says, it is a proven scientific fact that homosexuality does happen in almost all animal species.

Gay animals?

When people say, "You ain't normal 'cause you sure don't see no queer animals," they are just showing their ignorance. Both wild and domesticated animals have been having lesbian and gay relationships for as long as we've been watching them. It's just that most people don't like to mention it.

The first study on this was done over seventy-five years ago, but the findings were censored by the scientific community. Whether this was because of their own homophobia is unknown. What is known, and has been written up many times in scientific journals, is the fact that homo animals do exist.

The wild gay kingdom

Scientists have observed gay behavior in animals for centuries, but many were afraid to report their observations for fear of recrimination from a sometimes homophobic academia. Because of this fear, only a few intensive studies have been done. A recent ten-year study by a British scholar named Bruce Bagemihl resulted in proof that over 470 species of animals participate in homosexual relationships.

Bagemihl's 768-page book, *Biological Exuberance: Animal Homosexuality and Natural Diversity,* describes in detail, with many photos, male ostriches courting each other; lesbian sea gulls sharing nests and raising chicks together; male orangutans practicing fellatio (going down on each other); female long-eared hedgehog couples performing 69 together; male giraffes necking, mounting, and having orgasms; and hundreds of other animals such as penguins, walruses, whales, dolphins, mountain sheep, and vampire bats all documented as having same-sex relationships.

Like many people, some scientists are uncomfortable with the idea that every kind of same-sex activity known to be practiced by humans also exists in the animal kingdom. Some will argue that homosexual activities in animals are only dominance behaviors, or a behavior to make the animal's heterosexual partner jealous (that one seems like a bit of a stretch to me), but it is proven fact that same-sex behavior in animals is as natural as heterosexual behavior. The sad part is that humans are the only "animals" who respond with hostility towards same-sex behaviors in their society.

There is one homosexual animal tribe that cannot be denied by anyone who studies sexual behavior. The Bonobo, or pygmy chimpanzees, are famous for their love of same-sex activities. The females will sit face to face practicing tribadism (mutual genital rubbing) and the males are commonly seen French kissing while massaging each other's genitals. Many scientists feel that the Bonobos practice homosexuality as a way to have a more harmonious society. "Make Love Not War" seems to be their adage.

Hmmm, I'm wondering if that kind of "love each other, treat each other equal" attitude would help us humans? Maybe we should be a little more like the Bonobos, or some of the other animals, who don't seem to judge their fellow creatures for being who they really are.

Domesticated gay horses, cows, cats, and dogs

Before more scientific ways of telling when a female was coming into heat, farmers watched the behaviors of masculine cows and mares to let them know. Some used a chalk belly band on the cows, and when Elsie mounted her lovely girlfriend, leaving a nice chalk mark on her back, the farmer knew it was time for Claire to be bred. Many mares will not tolerate a stallion near them, and have to be artificially inseminated. These mares are usually quite butch-looking and will herd and mount other mares as a stallion would.

The sad thing is that, like us, many gay animals pay for how they are with abuse or even their lives. Take the case in Orlando, Florida where the guy beat his dog to death because he caught him humping on another male. Maybe that dog was gay, or maybe he was just showing the other dog who was the more dominant of the two, but the point is this. Did the dog who humped the other male love his owner any less? Did that one incident make all the good things he did while on this earth suddenly disappear? He will never fetch another ball, or bring joy by playing chase with a child because his owner was homophobic. Did the dog suddenly choose to be gay, or was he hiding it all along? When the opportunity arose, he did what his nature told him to and he lost his life over it. Sounds the same as all the other anti-gay crimes, except that most of our beatings, maimings, and killings get far less press coverage.

Being lesbian, choice, heredity, or a result of environment?

When I was younger, I used to think it was totally a soul choice to be gay, like you decided this before you came here to learn lessons from it. But then I realized the following similarities in several families with gay children:

1. A high school friend of mine had four kids in her family. Two of them are gay, and I always felt their mother was too. When the oldest sibling came out, the mother had a very hard time with it. In the middle of a heated argument she blurted out "If I can change then so can you!"

2. Several years later I befriended someone who has four brothers and sisters. Four out of the five siblings in this family are gay, and their mother kissed me right on the mouth one night! This same friend is with a woman whose sister is also lesbian. Years ago the sister, who is very butch, was with a fem guy who was going through sex reassignment surgery. Before the surgery was complete, the lesbian ended up pregnant. The couple had a baby who turned out gay.

3. Another friend of mine's father is gay, and so are both his sisters. Their father was known to have a "best friend" who was with him all the time, even though he was married.

4. Another lesbian I knew had a similar situation. Her mother repeatedly accused her father of being gay, because he had little interest in being sexual with her. After years of sneaking around and making it with guys, the father died of AIDS.

The last two stories knock out the theory that the gay gene is from the mother, because both the mothers mentioned are totally straight. Too bad. Can't blame women for this one!

Makes you think, doesn't it? Maybe it really is a combination of heredity, soul, and environment. Whatever it is, it is certainly not a choice. Who would choose to be persecuted, hated and called names, not trusted, accused of being a child molester, and possibly end up murdered? Not anyone that I know.

Think about this while you read the next chapter.

CHAPTER 7

Living in the primarily heterosexual USA

Our "civil rights" in the USA

Many people think that you cannot be discriminated against in housing, public accommodations, education, or employment if you are a gay man or woman. WRONG. I have been harassed by neighbors; told there were no vacancies at motels, even though their glaring neon sign said differently; advised not to come out on campus or I might lose my grant; and I've been fired from three jobs for being a lesbian. These things have been pretty devastating, to say the least.

I even had one employer hire a private investigator to track me. I had worked for him for over two years, and I was up for a promotion to assistant manager. When the investigator verified that I was lesbian, I was fired without notice right in the middle of the '80s recession. I went from being the head buyer for a store to squeezing dogs' anal glands in a grooming parlor, Of course my employers did not say my sexuality was the reason. No, they said I was a drug user, which was totally untrue—I don't even drink—and that I was "an unreliable employee." Hmmm. I guess never being late to work or missing a day in two years means unreliable to some people.

Now, you must remember this was in the deep South, where intolerance is a daily right to every god-fearin' homophobe, but there are people like this everywhere you go—people who are pointing one finger at you with three pointing right back at themselves!

Don't laws protect us from discrimination?

Not in most states, but most everyone I've spoken to thinks we are protected. An acquaintance of mine who has a doctorate said, "If I got fired I'd go to the Lambda Legal Defense and Educational Fund and get them to help me."

The Lambda Legal Defense Fund is a great organization, but there is little chance that they would be able to do anything, unless you are in one of the twenty-one states that has civil rights legislation for gay people written into their laws.

Those states are as follows: California, Colorado, Connecticut, Delaware, Hawaii, Illinois, Indiana, Maryland, Massachusetts, Minnesota, Montana, Nevada, New Hampshire, New Jersey, New Mexico, New York, Pennsylvania, Rhode Island, Vermont, Washington, Wisconsin. Of the twenty-one only Connecticut, Massachusetts, Vermont, and Wisconsin have

---

Native American Gay People

Over thirty different Native American tribes had a special position for women who showed masculine traits and skills. The Mohave called these women "hwame." They would be tested when they were children and upon passing the test, a ceremony would be performed which included taking on a masculine name, wearing masculine clothing, and learning how to use weapons for both hunting and protection. They would marry women as adults, and perform as warriors. Over 130 tribes had "berdaches," which were men who wore women's clothing. These men were usually given a ritual test when they started exhibiting feminine traits as children. If they passed the test, then they would be given female clothing and there would be a ceremony to announce their new female names. These men preformed women's chores and married other men. Many hwame and berdaches were thought to be great healers and were revered in their societies.

---

laws which prohibit discrimination based on sexual orientation in all categories. The categories are: public employment, public accommodations, private employment, education, housing, credit, and union practices. This information was compiled from the Lambda Defense and Educational Fund website and was last updated on January 4, 2002, so it may have changed by now.

If you want to live in a state that fully protects its gay citizens, then I'd say do some research on the ones listed above to make sure that the antidiscrimination laws have not been repealed or amended. Keep in mind that the laws are not going to change ignorant, intolerant people, and if you get into a lawsuit with a private individual, you can bet it will be a nasty fight to the bitter end.

There are also cities which have their own antidiscrimination laws. To see the summary of states, cities, and counties which prohibit discrimination based on sexual orientation go out on the Web to the Lambda Legal Defense and Educational Fund. (See the index for the Web address.)

Why aren't we protected? We pay taxes too!

Good question, but I cannot answer it. All I can say is, as you read this chapter, think about the fact that we, as lesbians, live in a "free country." Most of us work hard; make house payments or pay rent; support ourselves, pets, or kids, on salaries significantly below a "family man's" wage; and shell out much of our gross income to taxes.

The tax thing irritates me more than anything, so I am going to include a very loose approximation of how much gay people paid out in taxes for one year. The estimate was compiled from the website of the U.S. Census Bureau. The employment numbers available were for October 1, 2000. So here we go:

On October 1, 2000 there were approximately 162,410,000 people living in the USA between the ages of 20 and 64 years old (what I would consider working age). If you multiply that number by 10 percent (the low end of the approximate percentage of the population who are gay, both men and women) you get 16,241,000 gay people employed. If you take that number and multiply it by the median income (let's go way low to make up for the approximate number of gay people who may not be working, and say $20,000 per year) you get $324,820,000,000 in gay annual salaries, which we spend in the USA as consumers. Now multiply this by the federal tax rate of 12.5% (keep in mind, most of us pay almost 25% of our wages) and you get gay people paying $40,602,500,000 in federal income taxes per year. This does not include state or local taxes.

Now wait a minute! We pay over forty BILLION dollars in federal income taxes and yet we have no rights in many of the states across the United States? What's up with that? The only

---

A Personal Stand

I've been buying gas from a small, privately owned convenience store for the past six years, that is until I found out that the owner was sending homophobic hate letters to a church here in town who has opened its doors to gay people. I will never do business with his store again, which means $15.00 a week times 4 equals $60.00 a month, times 12 equals $720.00 a year of "Lesbyterian" money that he sure won't be getting! Now think about if every gay person in town who went to that gas station decided to make a personal stand—10 percent of the homophobe's income would suddenly disappear. "Hit 'em where it hurts," which to me means the ol' pocket. My gay gas dollars are now going to a station across town that employs an openly out attendant. Sure, I have to drive a little farther, but believe me it's worth it.

---

right the federal government gives us is that we cannot be discriminated against in public employment; but if someone wants to fire you, believe me, they'll find a way to get around that little law. Doesn't the *Pledge of Allegiance* say "and freedom and justice for all"? I don't think that pledge means freedom and justice just for straight, white Christians, especially since this country was founded on religious freedom for all who seek it.

Did You Know?

Katharine Lee Bates wrote "America the Beautiful" for the woman she had a loving relationship with for twenty-five years.

Now, I'm not trying to fuel the fire into a lesbian war, but this is just not right. I don't know what the solution is either. I did have a discussion with a black man who was running for senate in the state where I live. I told him how I felt I had no rights as a lesbian, and how I thought it was very similar to how black people had no rights just forty years ago. He sadly shook his head and replied, "The only thing I know to tell you to do is to make a stand for your own rights as an American. It's scary, but one person can make a difference." I think he was speaking from experience, being that he's black and was running for the senate in a state where many are racist.

I never forgot our little discussion, but for years I was unsure of how one person could do anything to change the way a whole country thinks. Then I read the book *Excuse Me, Your LIFE is Waiting*, and my whole way of viewing things turned around. I learned that the first step to figuring out what you want life to be is to know what you don't want or have. So, with that in mind, the next section will cover the basic things we don't have at this time because we were born lesbian and not heterosexual.

The privilege of being heterosexual

There are many privileges that people automatically have for being born heterosexual. Most are just so ingrained in all of us that we don't even question their validity, that is unless these privileges are taken away by homophobia.

Heterosexual Privilege #1: Marriage

When you are in a heterosexual marriage your relationship is happily supported by society. Holidays, vacations, and celebrations are promoted by parents, in-laws, coworkers, and most people in general. What you do to celebrate these occasions can be freely discussed without any fear of people scoffing at your most precious relationship.

When you are in a heterosexual marriage, you will automatically be able to sign up for certain types of insurance, such as homeowners, auto, or health at a reduced "family rate."

You will have full visitation rights in the hospital intensive care or ambulatory units, and be allowed to automatically make decisions for your spouse if she or he is incapacitated.

If your spouse becomes sick, or dies suddenly, you will probably receive paid leave from your job, no questions asked. The joint properties will automatically be turned over to the remaining spouse under probate laws, and you will

---

Personal Experience:

Because of the fact that we have no rights to visit or make life decisions if one of us is incapacitated in the hospital, my partner and I decided to get legal power of attorney for each other. This way if something happens we will have nearly the same control in decision making granted to married heterosexuals. If you are in a committed relationship, you should also both have a will drawn up specifying who receives the property if either of you has an untimely death.

Did You Know?

During ancient times in Europe, clergy regularly performed same-sex union ceremonies which were almost identical to heterosexual weddings? The only difference was that the same-sex unions were considered for love, and most of the heterosexual unions were for the joining of two high-powered families. The Roman soldiers Serge and Bacchus were joined in such a ceremony, and were executed after refusing to sacrifice to the emperor's idols. They were later pronounced Christian military saints.

---

receive Social Security benefits from your spouse's fund.

If you are married you may file joint tax returns and receive tax cuts that single people or single people in a committed relationship do not have.

If your marriage ends in divorce and there are children involved, you will probably have joint child custody, or at least visitation rights to your children. You will also have legal recourse to an attorney who can handle the separation of material goods if hard feelings exist.

Heterosexual Privilege #2: Total Cultural Acceptance

You will be able to live openly with your partner without fear of being an outcast in your neighborhood, work, or social life. You can freely discuss both the good and the bad times of your relationship with support from others. If you are still in high school you can automatically use the correct pronoun for the person you are dating, and not have to lie about who you went to the movies with on Saturday night. You will not have to explain your relationship to people who are just meeting you or make up a lie about who you really are. You will not have to wait to know new acquaintances a year before you disclose who your life partner is. You will not have to fear their possible rejection.

You will not have to worry about speaking to children in your neighborhood, for fear that their parents may be thinking you are trying to change them into something they may or may not already be, or trying to molest them. You will not have to be afraid for your life when walking to your car outside of the bar of your peers. You will not have to worry that homosexuals will come into the bar of your peers and harass or stare at you, come onto you, or cruise the parking lots outside and dent your car or slice the tires. You will not have to worry that if you tell someone you are heterosexual they could kidnap you from wherever you are, and beat, rape, or kill you.

Heterosexual Privilege #3: Being Viewed as "Normal"

Your whole life is not tainted by the nagging wonder of what might happen if so-and-so finds out? You will have wonderful role models in movies, on television, and in books that will teach you about romance and give you a very good idea of what a healthy heterosexual relationship is. You will be bombarded non-stop through the media with people you can identify with. You will not ever have to question your sexuality in relation to what society deems correct.

Heterosexual Privilege #4: Total Acceptance by Employers, Church, and State

If you are heterosexual, you will not have to worry about disclosing who you are in an interview for fear of not being hired. You will not have to guard your personal life fiercely, having little contact with coworkers and not attending company social activities in order to protect you job. You will not have to lie about who your beneficiary is on your life insurance policy, or choose a family member instead of the person you live with. You will not have to be on guard any time you are anywhere with your partner, for fear someone from work will see you and label you as a homosexual. You will not have to say your heterosexual boyfriend, girlfriend, wife or husband is "your friend," when introducing them to people from your work. You will not have to worry about

> **Personal Experience:**
>
> When my life-partner and I bought our house, we decided to use the same insurance company that was already covering it. We were blatantly turned down because we were two unmarried women living in a house together.

displaying affection to your significant other in public. You can openly have a job as a minister or a teacher without the constant worry of being humiliated and fired if your private life is discovered. You may openly adopt or provide foster care to children. In a divorce situation you can raise your own children without the constant threat that your ex will regain custody in a court of law because of who you love. You will not have to hide your relationship from the police if your children get in trouble. You will be able to openly serve in the military.

Heterosexism, a right of the majority?

At present, heterosexism is everywhere we look. From TV to billboards to advertising on the radio, we are constantly bombarded with heterosexual imagery, and yet we are still lesbian. Much time and research has been done on the question of human sexuality, and we are still shrugging our shoulders and scratching our heads.

Several years ago a questionnaire was distributed in hopes of getting answers to the age old question, "What makes a person gay?" Following is the lesbian version of that questionnaire.

Heterosexual, choice or not?

1. How old were you when you decided you were going to be a heterosexual?

2. Deep down inside, what do you believe converted you into a heterosexual?

3. Do you think you may grow out of being a heterosexual?

4. How do you know for sure that you are heterosexual if you have never had sexual relations with someone of your own sex?

5. Do you have a deep-seated fear of lesbians and gay men which causes you to be heterosexual?

6. Even though it is a fact that most child molesters are heterosexuals, do you still feel it is OK for your children to be taught by heterosexual teachers?

7. Even though society supports heterosexual marriage, it ends in divorce nearly 50 percent of the time. Why aren't heterosexuals content with their "preferred" lifestyle?

8. Do you believe you could be influenced and become a lesbian?

9. Do you think you will ever be a complete human being by limiting yourself and your sexuality to being only heterosexual?

10. Even though their lives will be plagued with problems, would you still want your children to be heterosexual?

11. Since most heterosexuals are so unhappy with their chosen lifestyle, perhaps some type of aversion therapy may help those who really want to become a happy productive, well-rounded person.

Hopefully, the questionnaire helped you to feel a little better about this chapter. I know sometimes it is easier to ignore the problems of being a gay woman or man in this culture, but that will not make them go away. The only way for change to happen is if we realize that there is something desperately wrong with how at least 10 percent of the population is being treated, and make a step for positive change. We need to stop judging each other, and take back the control of our thoughts, feelings, and lives instead. We need to learn how to feel what it would be like to have all the rights of our heterosexual sisters and brothers, in order to will our desires into change. It's called making plans. I know this can be difficult, but we all need to learn to think as positive as possible no matter what is going on. We also need to use good sense in finding support when we are feeling low.

Many of my straight friends have no idea how hard it can be to live as a lesbian today. They think because Ellen had a TV show that everything is good concerning lesbians and society. Many think because they accept us, everyone else will, which leads to them possibly blurting out who you are in the breakroom at work or the classroom at school. Many of my friends either do not understand the prejudices and intolerances that we face on a daily basis, or, because of heterosexual privilege, it just never crossed their minds.

The thing I have found that works best is to openly discuss unfair situations with your supportive straight friends. If you come out to people you trust, make sure to tell them that it has been your experience that not everyone views lesbians in a nice way. Some people can become so threatened that they could cause you to lose your job or even your housing. Help your heterosexual friends to understand that all is not bright and sunny on our side of the fence, and that we have plenty of sharp rocks and weeds to pull out before there are green pastures for us. I don't mean that you should dwell nonstop on the woes of being different, but if something has happened to you that is upsetting, don't just keep it in. You may be surprised at how your honesty can help your straight friends change into supporters who will stand up for the rights of all gay people, not tolerate lesbian or gay jokes or slurs, and basically dig up a hidden cactus before you even come close to stepping on it.

If you are having trouble coping with life in general and feel you need a bit of professional help, be sure to check out Chapter 10. If you would like to learn more about what your thoughts and feelings can do for you, see the index for information on the book *Excuse Me, Your LIFE is Waiting.*

CHAPTER 8

Our own role models

Most everyone needs a role model, someone she can look up to who has similar traits, someone who has survived the tough times and stands as a symbol of our culture. When I started doing the research for this chapter I was surprised because there are many famous gay and bisexual people throughout history, but very few people realized or admitted it. Because of the time periods some lived in, many of the people listed in this chapter were not "out," but their deep involvement and love of one dear friend of the same sex led biographers to speculate that they were indeed lesbian or gay.

The people included in this chapter are just a few of the thousands of gay women and men who have paved the way for the rest of us. If someone is offended because their distant closeted relatives are included in this section, please accept my apologies in advance. I don't wish to hurt anyone, just bring a little pride to noteworthy people whose love may have never been recognized before.

Famous lesbians and bi women then and now

Jane Addams, an author who was publicly out in the 1880s, and the first woman president of the National Conference of Social Work, was born in Cedarville, Illinois in 1860. She attended Rockland College and after graduation went to the Women's Medical College in Philadelphia. She traveled in Europe with a close companion, Ellen Gates Starr. The two founded the Hull House, a place where young social workers could be trained. Hull House grew into a campus that featured college classes; training in music, art and theatre; and work training including a children's nursery, playgrounds, and a large community kitchen. Jane fell in love with Mary Rozet

Smith and the two bought a house and were together for forty years. When traveling they always requested a single bed instead of the appropriate double beds for two women.

Susan B. Anthony, powerful cofounder of the Women's Rights movement, was born in 1820. Susan B. Anthony was one of the first leaders for the rights of women in regards to owning, managing or inheriting property, and having custody of their children. In 1851 she met Elizabeth Cady Stanton, another women's rights campaigner. The two had a personal and political partnership for fifty years, which Susan called "a natural union of head and heart." It is unknown if the married Elizabeth Stanton and Susan B. Anthony had a physical relationship, but their political vision, loyalty to the cause and one another, and their daring actions made them one of the greatest couples of the nineteenth century. In 1868 Susan met Anna Dickinson, and it is said that the two had a passionate relationship. In 1872 Susan registered and voted illegally in Rochester, New York. She was arrested and fined, but she refused to pay. The publicity about the outrage of women helped in the fight for women's rights, and in 1906 the so-called "Anthony Amendment," which is known today as the nineteenth amendment, granted women full suffrage.

Katharine Lee Bates, author of the song "America the Beautiful," was born in 1859. As a young woman she attended Wellesley College. After her graduation she became a faculty member there. She became friends with a colleague, Katharine Coman. The two had a relationship for twenty-five years, and Bates wrote many poems about their love. It is said that Bates wrote "America the Beautiful" for Katharine Coman while traveling cross-country in a Conestoga wagon. Pretty amazing that this song of national pride was written by a probable lesbian.

Marie-Rosalie Bonheur, famous French painter, was born in Bordeaux in 1822. Both of her parents were involved heavily in the artistic and musical movement of that time. They believed in supporting creative endeavors, and all four of their children became artists. Rosa studied in Paris and specialized in painting animals. Her painting *The Horse Fair* was bought by Cornelius Vanderbilt for the record sum of 4,200 franks. She smoked cigarettes and wore men's clothing. She fell in love with Nathalie Micas and they lived together until Nathalie's death. Sometime later, Rosa met an American artist named Anna Elizabeth Klumpke. The two fell in love and were together for the rest of their lives. Rosa, Nathalie and Elizabeth were all buried together beneath the inscription "Friendship is divine affection."

Rita Mae Brown, author of one of the first lesbian novels with a positive ending, was born in 1944. Rita Mae Brown was adopted as an infant and raised in Fort Lauderdale Florida. She is a well-known lesbian, feminist, and activist. Her first novel, *Rubyfruit Jungle*, was handled through a small press, Daughters Inc. It sold over seventy thousand copies, proving that a lesbian novel could be successful. In 1977 Bantam Books bought the rights for *Rubyfruit Jungle* for $250,000 and had 300,000 copies printed. Since that time, Rita Mae Brown has written many wonderful books, including two of my all-time favorites, *Six of One* and *Southern Discomfort*. She has worked as a screenwriter in Los Angeles, and she was nominated for two Emmys. She has had relationships with other well-known lesbians such as Martina Navratilova and Martina's ex-lover, Judy Nelson.

Ellen DeGeneres, a comedian with her own weekly sitcom, was born in 1958 in Louisiana. She was the first lesbian to portray a main character on a prime-time television show coming to terms with her own sexuality. Even though the first *Ellen* show was canceled, it opened the doors of communication for many people dealing with their own issues of being lesbian. I had one friend who watched the famous coming out episode with her mother. Afterwards her mother turned to her and asked "Well, is there something you want to tell me?" which opened the doors of positive communication in that family. Ellen has since been in several films, and she starred in her own HBO comedy show. She had a very public three-year relationship with actress, Anne Heche. Both appeared on many talk shows in support of lesbian rights, including the *Oprah* show.

Emily Dickinson, a secretive and reclusive poet, was born in 1830. Raised in Amherst, Massachusetts, Emily went to college at Amherst Academy and then attended Mount Holyoke College. Both schools were Christian in nature, but Emily could not publicly testify to her belief in the religion and left Mount Holyoke after a year. She began writing poetry and traveled for a while, but then started to have problems with her eyes. She came back to the family home and became more and more reclusive. During these times she wrote letters and poetry to people she cared about. Many of her friends tried to get her to publish her poetry, but she would have none of it. Maybe it was her intense privacy issues or maybe it was the fact that she wrote hundreds of passionate poems about Susan Gilbert, a close friend who later became Emily's sister-in-law. After Susan's marriage to Austin Dickinson, Emily stopped writing to her. She did continue writing poems about women, all of which were hidden in her bedroom that she hardly strayed from. Upon Emily's death, over one thousand poems were found in her bureau, but all of

Susan's letters were destroyed. It will never be known what Susan felt for Emily, or how she handled such amorous advances from another woman. A few selected poems were published right after Emily's death, and in 1955 the entire collection was published.

Melissa Etheridge, one of the first mainstream lesbian singer/songwriters, who also plays a mean guitar, was born in Leavenworth, Kansas, in 1961. Melissa married Hollywood director Julie Cypher. Deciding to have children, the couple asked their friend, David Crosby, to be a sperm donor. He agreed and Julie had a baby girl. Several years later she had a baby boy. In 1999 Melissa and Julie received GLAAD's Stephen F. Kolzak Award. The award is given to openly lesbian or gay individuals in the media for outstanding contribution in combating homophobia. Melissa and Julie's public relationship went on for twelve years only to end amicably in 2000. Both women still feel that raising their children is the most important thing to do. Melissa also hosts a TV program called *Beyond Chance*—a show filled with strange, positive miracles which happen to ordinary people.

Anna Freud, daughter of Sigmund Freud, was born in 1895 in Vienna, Austria. Throughout her life, she was exposed to discussions of psychology, and after teaching elementary school for several years, she decided to enter the field of child psychology. She opened a practice and treated the children of Dorothy Burlingham, who was separated from her husband. Anna and Dorothy fell in love and had a lifelong relationship. The two began the Hampstead War Nurseries for children who had been separated from their families during World War II, and in 1952 they opened the Hampstead Child Therapy Course and Clinic. Whether the two had a physical relationship is unknown, but they had a passionate intellectual connection that precluded any other relationships with men.

Radclyffe Hall was a radical butch writer whose lesbian book, *The Well of Loneliness*, was banned in London. Born to wealthy English parents in 1880, Radclyffe was an out lesbian from the start. She wore men's clothes, sported a short haircut, and enjoyed fast cars, fox hunting, and women. Known to her friends as John, Radclyffe was said to have been with more women than she had read books. When she was 27, Radclyffe fell in love with Mabel Batten. Mabel was in her late forties when they moved in together. Their affair ended eight years later when Mabel dropped dead of a heart attack. The two were arguing over Radclyffe's close friendship with Una Troubridge. Una and Radclyffe later became lovers and stayed together for the next thirty years.

k.d. lang, wild lesbian country singer, was born in Canada in 1961. Her amazing voice lent itself to many types of music, but country was her choice. She was discovered and accepted as a country star, that is until she came out as a vegetarian, animal rights activist, and then as a lesbian. k.d.'s country career floundered, but her voice rang true and she moved into pop music. She costarred in the movie *Salmonberries* and provided most of the soundtrack. She was one of the first internationally known musical performers to come out, and k.d. was presented the *Creative Integrity Award* at Women's Night by Ellen DeGeneres in 1997.

Martina Navratilova, astonishing lesbian tennis athlete, was born in Czechoslovakia in 1956. Her mother was a ski instructor, and her stepfather was a tennis instructor who encouraged Martina to take up the sport. She started playing tournaments at a young age. After years of turning over her winnings to the Czechoslovakian Tennis Federation, Martina defected. Soon after coming to live in the U.S., Martina discovered her attraction to women. She had relationships with her manager, Sandra Haynie, novelist Rita Mae Brown, and Judy Nelson. Even though her private life has been smeared constantly by the press, Martina has become an incredible supporter for the rights of all gay people. She agreed to be the unpaid spokesperson for the Rainbow credit card, which helps fund causes such as the National Center for Lesbian Rights and the Community Research Initiative on AIDS. She has been called "The most gifted and incredible tennis player in the world," and has won eighteen Grand Slam singles titles along with thirty-one doubles titles. She set a record in 1984 by winning seventy-four straight singles matches, and she has been ranked number one in the world seven times.

Florence Nightingale, a lesbian who was chosen by God to devote her life to service, was born in Florence, Italy in 1820. At the age of seventeen, Florence said she heard God's voice, although she didn't quite know what he meant by "service." It took her nine years to figure it out. During this time she fell ill and was nursed back to health by her aunt. The two became passionate friends, but it is not known if their friendship was physical or not. During the 1840s, Florence fell in love with her cousin, Marianne Nicholson. Marianne's brother fell in love with Florence and eventually proposed, but he was turned down. Marianne was infuriated and Florence was devastated. She turned her passion into studying public health and hospitals and trained as a nurse. Florence took charge of nursing in the British military hospital during the Crimean War. She revamped the way the hospital was run. In 1860 she organized the first school of nursing in London, England, and became an expert in health and sanitation.

Eleanor Roosevelt, the most controversial first lady of the U.S., and a supporter of women's rights, world peace, and a lesbian's right to privacy, was born in New York City in 1884. Eleanor Roosevelt was orphaned at age nine. She was raised by her grandmother and married her fifth cousin, Franklin Delano Roosevelt. She had six children. She gave the first press conference by a president's wife and wrote a newspaper column titled "My Day," which focused on social problems of the underprivileged. Appointed as assistant director of defense, Eleanor traveled the world. She had several friendships with lesbian couples and a passionate love affair with lesbian reporter Lorena Hickock. Upon Lorena's death, many of their love letters were mysteriously destroyed, but the few that remain show a loving relationship between two very private women.

Sappho, the first publicly outspoken woman who openly loved women, was born in 610 B.C. on the Aegean island of Lesbos. Married to a wealthy merchant, Sappho had a daughter and spent time reciting poetry at all-women poetry readings. She wrote passionate lyrical poetry concerning her love for and attraction to other women. She was known as one of the greatest Greek lyrical poets, and people traveled from great distances to hear her perform.

Bessie Smith, blues singer extraordinaire, was born in 1894 in Chattanooga, Tennessee. Bessie Smith is one of the most famous blues singers of all time. She sang with Ma Rainey, who was blamed for bringing Bessie into the lesbian fold. Her first recording, "Downhearted Blues," sold more copies than any other blues singer of her time. Bessie was married to Jack Gee, but she was constantly enraging him with her blatant affairs with women, including one with Lillian Simpson, a chorus girl in Bessie's touring show. Bessie frequented wild parties where same-sex couples openly danced and practiced "heavy petting." She traveled the U.S. extensively, performing in all sorts of venues, and was known to have fought off the KKK at one of her shows.

Gertrude Stein, fabulous lesbian, feminist, novelist and poet, was born in Allegheny, Pennsylvania in 1874. She studied psychology at Radcliffe College, and attended John Hopkins Medical School, but decided on literature as a career. She had an affair with May Bookstaver, who inspired Gertrude to write a novel entitled *Q.E.D.* Gertrude never allowed this book to be published as it was explicitly lesbian in nature. Gertrude had code words in her writing, such as "have a cow," which meant a woman having an orgasm. Gertrude met Alice B. Toklas in 1907, and the two fell in love and became lifetime companions. Gertrude and Alice were the most famous lesbian couple of their time. Their classic butch/femme relationship may be why we still have stereotypes of lesbian relationships to this day.

Alice Walker, African-American feminist writer, was born in 1944 in Eatonton, Georgia. An avowed bisexual, Alice is best known for her Pulitzer Prize-winning novel *The Color Purple*. Her other works include *You Can't Keep a Good Woman Down*, *Revolutionary Petunias*, *In Search of Our Mothers' Gardens*, *To Hell With Dying*, *Meridian*, *Possessing the Secret of Joy*, and *The Temple of My Familiar*.

Patricia Nell Warren, lesbian author and gay rights activist, was born in Helena, Montana in 1936. She attended Stephens College, in Columbia, Missouri, and went on to Manhattanville College in Purchase, New York, where she received her B.S. in English literature. From 1959 to 1981 she worked as an editor for *Reader's Digest*. She wrote the first breakthrough gay novel in the early seventies, *The Front Runner*, which made the *New York Times*' bestseller list in 1974 and has continued to be one of the top-selling gay novels of all time. Her book *The Beauty Queen* was the first book I ever read that had gay and lesbian characters. Patricia has written several other bestsellers and published four books of poetry. She has an estimated 20 million readers. Her poems, articles, and essays have appeared in *The Advocate*, *Genre*, *Lesbian News*, *Harvard Gay and Lesbian Review*, *Philadelphia Gay News*, *Lifestyle*, as well as *Modern Maturity*, *Atlantic Monthly*, the *Los Angeles Times*, *Prairie Schooner*, *Reader's Digest*, *San Francisco Chronicle*, *Persimmon Hill*, and *American West*.

Patricia is also involved with gay and lesbian youth, and has lectured at schools and colleges across the U.S. She has done volunteer teaching in Los Angeles' well-known gay and lesbian high school, EAGLES Center. Patricia is a wonderful person who helps people in any way she can. I should know, she's been my mentor for several years.

Virginia Woolf, a home-schooled writer who found the idea of sex with a man distasteful, was born in London, England in 1882. She survived several nervous breakdowns which began at the age of 13 with her mother's death. She married an art critic and started the Bloomsberry Group, which consisted of several homosexuals and a few open-minded straights. After her divorce, she married again and produced several novels. The stress was rising in her life again, and she succumbed to yet another nervous breakdown. In 1922 she fell in love with Vita Sackville West. Their relationship lasted many years, and during this time Virginia wrote *Orlando* as a gift to her lover. She wrote many remarkable essays including *A Room of One's Own* and *Three Guineas*, but lost her battle with depression when she took her own life in the River Ouse in 1941.

The Woman Chief of the Crow Indians was the only name this nineteenth century lesbian Plains Indian was known by. Kidnapped by the Crow at age ten, the young girl was adopted and raised buy a Crow warrior. When she showed an interest in manly deeds, her foster father encouraged her by giving her bows and arrows and teaching her to ride horses as if a warrior. As she grew up, she bettered most of the young men in her tribe in manly sports. She could handle a gun or bows and arrows, and spent much time hunting bighorns and deer, which she butchered and then carried back to the tribe on her back. She lead a successful counterattack against the Blackfeet,which made her a heroine to the Crow Nation, and was later ranked as third person in the band of 160 lodges. She soon married a woman, and then went on to marry three more. For twenty years she lived as a Crow chief until 1854 when she was killed on a peacemaking journey.

Some famous gay male role models

Since this is a book about lesbians, I decided to just list the famous gay and bi guys:

Alexander The Great, St. Augustine, Lord George Gordon Byron, Michelangelo Buonarroti, Leonardo Da Vinci, David and Jonathon (from the Old Testament), King Edward II, Rock Hudson, King James I, Freddie Mercury, Harvey Milk, King Richard the Lionhearted, Saints Serge and Bacchus who were joined in a holy union, William Shakespeare, Socrates, Peter Tchaikovsky, Andy Warhol, Walt Whitman, Oscar Wilde, King William II, King William III, Tennessee Williams, and Wladziu Liberace, to name a few.

Heros for us all

I also wanted to include two brave gay men who were heros in the tragic attacks in the United States on September 11, 2001. They are as follows:

Mark Bingham, a rugby player from San Francisco, was one of the people who overpowered the hijackers on Flight 93 and successfully thwarted their next target, which was speculated to have been the White House.

Father Mychal Judge, a NYC fire department chaplin, was struck down while giving last rites to victims at ground zero.

I am sure there were many more lesbian and gay heros in the horrible tragedy of September 11th, but as shown in this chapter our stories are seldom told.

It saddened me to know that the people who loved the men mentioned above were not honored in a ceremony at the White House. Maybe it is just too much for most people to realize that we can be brave and valiant; maybe it was too hard to know that some of us would sacrifice our lives to save thousands of others, or that we could walk into the mouth of hell to hold the hand of a dying brother or sister while knowing that death was looming over us in a building soon to collapse.

My heart goes out to all of you who lost loved ones in the tragedy. My love goes out to all the gay men and women who sat alone with their grief with little support because of who they are in this life.

Be strong and proud

Even though many of our stories and accomplishments have been dismissed throughout history, I hope this chapter helps you feel good about who we are as lesbians. Stand tall with your head held high, because we have some great people on our side of the fence.

CHAPTER 9

Lesbian fiction and film

Books and films are an important part of our world. Sometimes they represent the true heart and feelings about what is going on during a certain time in history. In the beginning, lesbians and gay men were usually portrayed as emotionally sick and full of self-loathing in both books and film. Today, books have gone past that image, although most mainstream films are still lagging behind.

I'm not talking about the wonderful independent films that are winning awards at film festivals across the world and being viewed in arty film houses. What I am talking about are the films featuring lesbians as main characters done by big Hollywood studios. Almost all of these still portray lesbians as drug addicts, killers, thieves, suicidal, or confused women who, after some hot love scene with a lesbian, come to their senses and fall into the first straight man's arms they can find. I can only think of one mainstream film, with well-known actresses, where the two women literally went off into the sunset on a bus. Of course they went off with a bunch of illegal money from a laundering scam, but hey, that's better than them dying tragic deaths like most of the others.

It is time for a change—for us to be viewed as we really are. Not as some desperate sex-crazed dykes who would kill you in a second for money or drugs. Maybe it is because our lives are so normal that it just doesn't make good fiction, but I don't believe that. For homophobia to decrease, people need to realize that we are pretty much the same as anyone else. Working hard, paying bills, and living day to day. If we are viewed as the scourge of society, it gives that same society a reason to believe all the false stereotypes that they have been fed for years.

Now I know that there are huge financial reasons for having high drama on the lesbian prairie. I realized this hard fact when my partner and I went to see *Philadelphia* and half the people in the theatre walked out when the two guys kissed. The good thing is I do see a change eventually happening. With the increase of somewhat normal gay and lesbian characters on TV, featured on shows like *Will & Grace* and *ER*, more people will be exposed to the fact that we are not all sick pervs trying to seduce straight guys' wives or children.

Some of the top lesbian films

Below is a list of some of the best films which deal with lesbianism. Most have been compiled by Raymond Murray, author of *Images in the Dark: An Encyclopedia of Gay and Lesbian Film and Video*. Mr. Murray is also the founder and president of TLA Video, a wonderful company which features "hip, foreign, alternative movies"; among these are hundreds of movies featuring gay women and men. TLA has six stores and a huge website where you can buy these great movies without the hassle of ordering from a local, sometimes homophobic, video store (see the index for more info). Thanks to Mr. Murray for giving me permission to use his great reviews.

Aimee & Jaguar (1999, 126 min, Germany)
Director: Max Farberbock   Studio: Zeitgeist
Starring: Maria Schrader, Juliane Kohler, Johana Wokalek, Heike Makatsch
Aimee & Jaguar is a rare film. It leaves the audience weeping about the dire consequences an intense love has wrought, but exhilarated over the existence of such love. Aimee tells the true story of Lilly

(Kohler) and Felice (Schrader), lovers in WWII Germany. Lilly is married to a Nazi officer, away at the front, and she has many affairs while her husband is gone. Felice is the leading light of her circle of lesbians, in love with Ilse (Wokalek), but smitten with Lilly. Felice knows that the relationship is impossible, but she doesn't care. She's headstrong and she's met her soul mate. Felice is not only a lesbian, but Jewish as well . . . prime target for the Nazis to ship off to the camps. The story is told through flashbacks when Lilly is an old woman being brought to a retirement home where she happens to meet another of their circle from the war. (This video is currently out of print and is not available for sale, but may possibly be found for rent.)

All Over Me (1997, 90 min, U.S.)
Director: Alex Sichel   Studio: New Line
Starring: Alison Follard, Tara Subkoff, Wilson Cruz,
Cole Hauser, Leisha Haley
This independently made film wonderfully captures the growing pains of adolescence and the joy, tentativeness, and excitement of a gawky teenager's emerging lesbian identity. Set in New York's Hell's Kitchen area, the story focuses on Claude (Alison Follard) and her best friend Ellen (Tara Subkoff). Claude feels completely alone, suffering not only from the typical neuroses of adolescence but from her unrequited love for Ellen, who is enthusiastically straight. Moody and uncommunicative, Claude eventually finds solace with a wannabe riot girl and fellow baby dyke, Lucy. This is a story about change, separation, and self-discovery that is both knowing and sensitive.

Antonia's Line (1995, 93 min, The Netherlands)
Director: Marleen Gorris   Studio: Fox Lorber
Starring: Willeke van Ammelrooy, Els Dottermans,
Veere Van Overloop
A celebration of the love, unity, and strength of women, this

touching family chronicle/fable from lesbian director Gorris centers on four generations of women. The story, set in a small Dutch village, spans decades—from the devastation of the post-war period to the present—and follows the fiercely independent-minded Antonia (Willeke van Ammelrooy), who returns to her childhood farmhouse to till the soil and raise a family; all without the aid of the misogynistic townsfolk, a hypocritical church, and the often violence-prone men. Antonia is aided by her lesbian daughter, a granddaughter, and great-granddaughter and a group of social rejects who flock to her. This Oscar-winning Best Foreign Film is masterful storytelling that enthralls. (Dutch with English subtitles)

Bar Girls (1995, 95 min, U.S.)
Director: Marita Giovanni   Studio: MGM
Starring: Nancy Allison Wolfe, Lisa Parker,
Camile Griggs, Paula Sorge, Justine Slater

The mating rites and the accompanying mind games of L.A. lesbians are uncovered in this knowing romantic comedy. Lauran Hoffman's script (based on her autobiographical play) centers most of the action at the West Hollywood Girl Bar where "love" comes easy and often for its denizens. Loretta (Nancy Allison Wolfe), a writer and one of the bar's bed-hopping regulars, meets and all-too-quickly falls for the self-assured Rachel (Liza D'Agnostino), a bewitching aspiring actress. Their union is threatened, however, when J.R. (Camilla Riggs), an attractive butch cop, enters the scene. The sex-induced theatrics of these and other characters are detailed in both a humorous and dramatic fashion. (This video is currently out of print and is not available for sale, but may possibly be found for rent.)

Basic Instinct (1992, 127 min, U.S.)
Director: Paul Verhoeven   Studio: Artisan
Starring: Michael Douglas, Sharon Stone, Jeanne Tripplehorn,
George Dzunda, Dorothy Malone

When it opened at theatres, this thriller was surrounded by controversy for it raised a red flag for gays, lesbians, and feminists with its shockingly "retro" stereotypes of man-hating lesbians with a "basic instinct" for murder. The film follows Michael Douglas as a burned-out cop who falls in "lust" with the prime suspect in a series of brutal ice pick murders, lasciviously portrayed by Sharon Stone. *Basic Instinct* is seen by some as the despicable leader of "the lesbian as killer" genre, and others view it as a sexy tale of a lesbian who enjoys the pleasure of other women as well as sticking ice picks into men.

Better Than Chocolate (1999, 98 min, Canada)
Director: Anne Wheeler   Studio: Trimark/Trimark
Starring: Wendy Crewson, Karyn Dwyer, Christina Cox,
Anne-Marie MacDonald, Peter Outerbridge, Marya Delver,
Kevin Mundy, Tony Nappo, Jay Brazeau

Winner of Audience Awards in the Philadelphia, London and Toronto Gay and Lesbian Film Festivals, this enjoyable tale tells of lesbian love winning against all the odds. When 19-year-old Maggie's mother calls and says she is moving in, Maggie, who quit law school and has been sleeping on the couch at the lesbian book store, must find a sublet apartment and make it livable fast. To complicate matters, she has just met Kim, an artistic road warrior who has rolled into town and moved into both Maggie's heart and her new home. But Maggie hasn't come out to her mother yet so it's time to hide the sex toys and "straighten up." Add to the picture her lovesick best friend Judy, a transsexual estranged from her family; her uptight lesbian boss; and Maggie's randy teen brother who gets a few lessons on life, and you get an entertaining romantic comedy of errors and the frailty of the human heart.

Bound (1996, 108 min, U.S.)
Director: Andy Wachowski & Larry Wachowski   Studio: Artisan
Starring: Jennifer Tilly, Gina Gershon, Joe Pantoliano

Gina Gershon and Jennifer Tilly star as neighbors who become lovers first, then partners in crime. The question in this film is who will betray whom. *Bound* is an unexpected accomplishment, stylishly shot and edge-of-your-seat tense. It is also a landmark for its depiction of its lesbian heroines.

Bound and Gagged—A Love Story (1993, 96 min, U.S.)
Director: Daniel Appleby   Studio: Image
Starring: Elizabeth Saltarrelli, Ginger Lynn Allen, Chris Denton, Karen Allen, Chris Mulkey
This frantic lesbian comedy is an amazingly self-assured independent feature. Cliff, a slacker loser, finds that his best friend Elizabeth, a fun-loving but irrational bisexual, is hopelessly in love with an abused woman (former porn queen Ginger Lynn Allen). Things get out of control leaving the love-lorn Elizabeth no option but to abduct her love and hit the road, roaming the Midwest in a queer Thelma and Louise fashion.

Boys Don't Cry (1999, 116 min, U.S.)
Director: Kimberly Peirce   Studio: Fox
Starring: Hilary Swank, Chloë Sevigny, Peter Sarsgaard, Brendan Sexton III, Alison Folland, Alicia Goranson, Matt McGrath
One of the best films of 1999, this fictionalized drama focuses on the tragic real-life story of Brandon Teena, a biological woman (Teena Brandon) who decided quite early to live her life as a man—a decision he paid for with his life. Hilary Swank, in an Oscar-winning performance, is riveting as Brandon, a sweet, but far-from-perfect 21-year-old drifter who just simply wanted to be a boy and love women. The harrowing tale follows Brandon as he befriends and moves in with a group of poor but fun-loving people. He also falls in love with Lana (Chloë Sevigny in an equally impressive performance), a tough-talking gal who finally meets a man who respects her and treats her right. But when Brandon is exposed as a woman, ignorance, fear, and homophobia drive two of her male friends to violently confront him.

Boys on the Side (1995, 117 min, U.S.)

Director: Herbert Ross   Studio: Warner
Starring: Whoopi Goldberg, Mary-Louise Parker, Drew Barrymore,
James Remar, Matthew McConaughey, Estelle Parsons, Billy Wirth

Whoopi Goldberg plays a lesbian who takes to the road with Drew Barrymore and Mary-Louise Parker in this life-affirming "Thelma and Louise + One" soap opera. Only problem with this free-wheeling comedy is that everyone gets laid except for our sweet Whoopi!

But I'm a Cheerleader (2000, 90 min, U.S.)

Director: Jamie Babbit   Studio: Universal
Starring: Natasha Lyonne, Mink Stole, Bud Cort,
RuPaul Charles, Cathy Moriarty, Clea DuVall

Poor Megan (Lyonne), she may be a pretty high schooler, model student, and cheerleader who's dating the captain of the football team, but her loving parents think otherwise. You see, she's a vegetarian, she doesn't like kissing her boyfriend, and one can't ignore those Melissa Etheridge records. Afraid that their daughter will fall in with the dark forces of same-sex love, she is quickly carted off to "True Directions," a scarily cheerful five-step de-homofication rehab camp. There she finds herself joined by a group of butch baby dykes, lipstick lesbians, and several queeny gay boys. Sapphic sparks fly when Megan locks eyes with Graham (DuVall), a tomboy beauty with no intention of going straight.

Celestial Clockwork (1994, 86 min, France/Venezuela)

Director: Fina Torres   Studio: Hallmark
Starring: Ariadna Gil, Arielle Dombasle, Evelyne Didi

In dusty Caracas, the lovely Ana suddenly comes to her senses at the altar and flees her stunned husband-to-be. She jumps aboard the next Paris-bound plane and takes up residence in a funky crash pad with her old friend Alma. Ana sets out to pursue her career as an operatic soloist, but along the way runs afoul of the immigration authorities and discovers her budding lesbianism, falling in love with an attractive high-tech psychoanalyst who interviews all her patients remotely by video. This film is a highly entertaining ride with Ana on her picaresque journey to self-fulfillment. (Spanish and French with English subtitles)

The Celluloid Closet (1995, 102 min, U.S.)
Director: Rob Epstein & Jeffrey Friedman   Studio: Columbia
Featuring: Lily Tomlin, Susan Sarandon, Whoopi Goldberg,
Shirley MacLaine, Tony Curtis, Tom Hanks, Gore Vidal,
Quentin Crisp

Inspired by the late Vito Russo's book on the depiction of homosexuality in Hollywood cinema, this documentary offers a candid mini-history of gays and lesbians on screen. *The Celluloid Closet* takes a chronological approach to the subject, offering clips from the turn of the century through the silents, to the effeminate caricatures of the 1930s, the pitiful homosexual of the 1950s and '60s, the violently deviant homosexual of the '70s and '80s, and concluding with the squeaky clean image of recent times. While encompassing in scope, the film is simplistic; however, *The Celluloid Closet* is more than recommended. For something deeper, it is best to also read Russo's book.

Chained Girls (1965, 62 min, U.S.)
Director: Joseph Mawra   Studio: Something Weird

This "lost" lesbian camp documentary is a priceless cinematic gem. Attempting to be objective about the "problem" of lesbianism, the film takes us to their lairs (bars, apartments, and Greenwich Village) to show us what these sexually deviant women do. There are hilarious statistics thrown in; explanations of the different types of lesbians and acted out scenes of seduction, indoctrination, and recruitment. Mothers hold hard to your daughters!

The Children's Hour (1961, 107 min, U.S.)

Director: William Wyler   Studio: Warner
Starring: Shirley MacLaine, Audrey Hepburn, James Garner,
Miriam Hopkins, Veronica Cartwright

Audrey Hepburn and Shirley MacLaine are teachers at an all-girls' boarding school. When a vindictive little girl accuses the two of having an affair, their lives are ruined after a self-righteous community believes the unsubstantiated allegations. However, the rumor also forces MacLaine to come to terms with her closeted lesbian feelings.

Chasing Amy (1997, 105 min, U.S.)

Director: Kevin Smith   Studio: Disney
Starring: Ben Affleck, Joey Lauren Adams, Jason Lee,
Dwight Ewell, Jason Mewes, Kevin Smith, Matt Damon

Chasing Amy makes the proposition that a seemingly well-adjusted lesbian, one who states repeatedly that she is a dyed-in-the-wool dyke, needs only a penis to make her embrace heterosexuality. Ben Affleck plays a comic book artist who meets a kindred spirit (Joey Lauren Adams). After a few platonic dates, he finally breaks down and confesses his love for her. At first angry, she soon declares similar feelings and they begin a relationship. That is, until he discovers her sordid, straight past, which he can't stop obsessing over. He then dumps her, while she tearfully pleas for forgiveness and understanding.

Claire of the Moon (1992, 106 min, U.S.)

Director: Nicole Conn   Studio: Fox Lorber
Starring: Trisha Todd, Karen Trumbo, Faith McDevitt

At an oceanside women writers' retreat in Oregon, Dr. Noel Benedict (Karen Trumbo), a brooding psychologist and lesbian author of "serious" books, finds herself rooming with her opposite—Claire (Trisha Wood), a willowy yet cynical straight blond woman who is determinedly messy and fun-loving. Their budding relationship becomes a tense and inadvertently amusing cat-and-mouse game as they alternately try to overcome their insecurities, accept their true feelings, and pounce on each other. *Claire of the Moon* is a drama of simmering female sexual desire and equally strong denial.

Daughters of Darkness (1971, 96 min, Belgium)
Director: Harry Kumel   Studio: Anchor Bay
Starring: Delphine Seyrig, Daniele Ouimet, John Karlen
One from the vaults! Delphine Seyrig stars as a Hungarian countess and present-day vampiress who, in order to continue her daily blood baths, must continually prowl for nubile virgins. Her blood-gathering soirees take her to Belgium where she, along with her lesbian secretary, seductively stalks the hotel for a quick fix. Campy, funny and erotic, this Gothic tale explores the darker side of sexuality with shocking frankness.

Desert Hearts (1985, 93 min, U.S.)
Director: Donna Deitch   Studio: MGM
Starring: Helen Shaver, Patrice Charbonneau,
Audra Lindley, Gwen Welles
An American lesbian classic, "Desert Hearts" was trail-blazing in its positive depiction of a love affair between two intelligent and attractive women. An uptight English professor travels to Reno to get a divorce (the film is set in 1959), and there meets a sexy, free-spirited sculptress. Their attraction for each other and their budding love is played out in a realistic, romantic, and all-together sensuous fashion.

Emmanuelle (dubbed) (1974, 94 min, France)
Director: Just Jaeckin   Studio: Fox Lorber
Starring: Sylvia Kristel, Alain Cuny
One of the most famous soft-core sex films to hit international screens, this chastely steamy tale of sexual experimentation is

now most memorable for its strong lesbian sub-plots. Emmanuelle, while liking the sex with her randy husband, also enjoys the pleasures of women-to-women intimacy.

Entre Nous (1983, 110 min, France)
Director: Diane Kurys   Studio: Fox Lorber
Starring: Miou-Miou, Isabelle Huppert, Guy Marchand
This moving drama tells of the intensely close friendship between two women. Isabella Huppert portrays Lena, a reticent housewife resigned to the numbing security of her husband and family. Through a chance encounter, she meets Madeleine (Miou-Miou), a vibrantly Bohemian sculptress whose love and companionship open the door to Lena's self-discovery. (French with English subtitles)

Even Cowgirls Get the Blues (1994, 100 min, U.S.)
Director; Gus Van Sant   Studio: New Line
Starring: Uma Thurman, John Hurt, Rain Phoenix,
Lorraine Brocco, Keanu Reeves, Crispin Glover, Roseanne,
Udo Kier, Faye Dunaway, Steve Buscemi
Gus Van Sant's infamous box office disaster isn't exactly faithful to the book, but the lesbian affair between Uma Thurman and Rain Phoenix makes it well worthwhile. Taken from Tom Robbin's 1976 hippie novel, the story features Thurman as a big-thumbed gal who uses her effective digit to thumb her way around the country meeting up with a series of loony characters. One of the more interesting ones is John Hurt as "The Countess."

Female Perversions (1996, 113 min, U.S./Germany)
Director: Susan Streitfeld   Studio: Trimark
Starring: Tilda Swinton, Amy Madigan, Karen Sillas,
Clancy Brown, Frances Fisher, Paulina Porizkova
Swinton stars as Eve, a high-profile lawyer preparing for an interview with the governor in the hopes of being appointed a judge. In the meantime, she must contend with her estranged,

kleptomaniac sister (Madigan), a workaholic boyfriend (Brown), a somewhat hesitant female lover (Sillas), and her own inner demons. While the lesbian angle is not the film's main thrust, it proves important to the heroine in her efforts to find solace.

The Fox (1967, 110 min, U.S.)
Director: Mark Rydell
Starring: Anne Heywood, Sandy Dennis, Keir Dullea
One of Hollywood's earliest attempts at handling lesbianism as a central theme, this somber drama, adapted from a D.H. Lawrence novella, gives us two women in love but at the same time shows that it is not all that fulfilling. What starts as isolated love for the two ends with defection and betrayal by one and death for the other. (This video is currently out of print and is not available for sale, but may possibly be found for rent.)

French Twist (1995, 100 min, France)
Director: Josiane Balasko   Studio: Disney/Miramax
Starring: Josiane Balasko, Victoria Abril, Alain Chabat
Victoria Abril is Loli, the dutiful, housebound Spanish wife of a boorish French real estate broker (Alain Chabat), who prides himself on his profusion of extramarital affairs. Marijo (Josiane Balasko), a cigar-smoking dyke from Paris, lands on their doorstep in the South of France in a broken-down VW minivan. After a bit of small talk, Marino makes a pass at Loli. Starved for the attention of her philandering husband, Loli responds warmly to these advances, much to his outrage. But when his indiscretions come to light the whole situation really blows up and Loli retaliates in a most unusual way. (French with English subtitles)

Gia (1998, 125 min, U.S.)
Director: Michael Cristofer   Studio: HBO
Starring: Angelina Jolie, Elizabeth Mitchell,
Kylie Travis, Mercedes Ruehl, Faye Dunaway

A mesmerizing, fact-based drama about the tragic life of bisexual supermodel Gia Carangi, Cristofer's mercurial film boasts a sensational performance by Jolie in the title role. Gia's rise and fall from an unruly Philadelphia teenager who becomes a top model to drug addict and AIDS victim makes for spellbinding viewing. As Gia seeks love and support from her mother (Ruehl) and her hesitant girlfriend Linda (Mitchell), she breaks all the rules, and everyone's heart. Cristofer's approach to the material is never melodramatic; however, he uses diary snippets and memories from those who knew her to depict Gia's fast life and untimely death.

Go Fish (1994, 85 min, U.S.)
Director: Rose Troche   Studio: MGM
Starring: Guinevere Turner, V.S. Brodie
Seriously cute and boyishly hip Max (Turner), after a drought of ten months, is looking for love. She possibly finds it in the person of Ely (V.S. Brodie), a semi-dorky, slightly older woman. How the two women meet, court, and get together is wonderfully handled in a light, effervescent fashion that paints a finely detailed and on-target picture of young lesbian life.

Henry & June (1990, 140 min, U.S.)
Director: Philip Kaufman   Studio: Universal
Starring: Fred Ward, Uma Thurman, Maria de Medeiros,
Richard E. Grant, Kevin Spacey
The first film to earn the MPAA's NC-17 rating, director Kaufman's steamy adaptation of Anaïs Nin's novel about the passionate love triangle between herself, writer Henry Miller, and his wife June is a glorious sexual and literary odyssey through the streets of 1930s Paris. Exquisitely photographed, "Henry & June" sumptuously evokes a frenzied carnival atmosphere and makes for an extraordinary, sensual cinematic experience.

High Art (1998, 102 min, U.S.)

Director: Lisa Cholodenko   Studio: USA Home Entertainment
Starring: Ally Sheedy, Dadha Mitchell, Patricia Clarkson,
Tammy Grimes, Bill Sage

Syd (Mitchell) is a straight, blond-haired woman working as an intern at a high-powered photo magazine. She finds her ticket to fame and lesbianism in the person of Lucy Berliner (Sheedy). Lucy is a burned-out ex-photographer, living a decadent, druggy life with Greta (Clarkson), a German actress. Syd's lesbian urges are kicked into overdrive as she becomes entranced with the cool, thin Lucy. Their relationship sparks Lucy's creative juices and offers a career opportunity for Syd. The only losers are their ex's. A film which offers intriguing ideas on the nature of love, drugs, and art.

The Hunger (1983, 99 min, GB)

Director: Tony Scott   Studio: MGM
Starring: Catherine Deneuve, Susan Sarandon,
David Bowie, Cliff DeYoung, Willem Dafoe

Catherine Deneuve stars as Miriam, an icy, elegant vampiress, thousands of years old, who goes on the prowl for a new mate after her 200-year lover (David Bowie) quickly ages. Her affections find their way to Sara (Susan Sarandon), a doctor who has written on the subject of accelerated aging. Dripping with cinematic style and chic sexual intrigue, *The Hunger* is both a chilling vampire tale and a sensuous drama of lesbian attraction and desire. The two sensually flirt, fall into each other's arms, and make love— and, of course, share blood.

If These Walls Could Talk 2 (2000, 92 min, U.S.)

Directors: Jane Anderson, Martha Coolidge & Anne Heche
Studio: HBO
Starring: Vanessa Redgrave, Marian Seldes, Elizabeth Perkins,
Paul Giamatti, Michelle Williams, Chloë Sevigny, Nia Long,
Natasha Lyonne, Amy Carlson, Sharon Stone, Ellen DeGeneres,

Kathy Najimy, Mitchell Anderson

Vanessa Redgrave won the Emmy for Best Supporting Actress for her performance in the first part of this terrific film. Where the original *Walls* dealt with three women each struggling with unwanted pregnancy, the sequel takes a private look at the lives of three lesbian couples during three different time periods in America: the '60s, '70s, and the new millennium. The common link is the house of the title: they all occupy it at one time or another. The year 1961 features Marian Seldes and Vanessa Redgrave as an older lesbian couple who have been together for fifty years. When Seldes dies of a stroke, Redgrave is forced to grieve in silence. As she is not "family" in the traditional sense, Redgrave is forced to endure the humiliation of Seldes' only family coming to claim the house and its contents for themselves. The year 1972 confronts peer pressure and sexual identity as Michelle Williams finds herself attracted to the "butch" Chloë Sevigny, much to the chagrin of her hippie friends. In the year 2000, the house is now occupied by lovers Ellen DeGeneres and Sharon Stone. Deeply in love, the only thing missing from their idyllic life is a child of their own. Making her directorial debut, Anne Heche conveys the couple's frustrations and hopes (with sperm donors, adoption agencies, etc.) in a manner sure to hit close to home for anyone who has faced the same trials.

The Incredibly True Adventure of Two Girls in Love (1995, 95 min, U.S.)

Director: Maria Maggenti   Studio: Warner
Starring: Laurel Holloman, Nicole Parker,
Maggie Moore, Kate Stafford

Randy (Laurel Holloman) is a white high school tomboy living with her lesbian aunt. Evie (Nicole Parker) is a beautiful and pampered black teenager from the right side of the tracks. They meet and love blossoms despite their differences. But trouble brews for the two as both of their families undertake to break the lovers apart.

I've Heard the Mermaids Singing (1987, 81 min, Canada)
Director: Patricia Rozema
Starring: Sheila McCarthy, Paule Baillargeon
Shelia McCarthy is enchanting as the romantically naive Polly, who becomes infatuated with her female boss in this whimsical comedy. Her boss, the curator of the gallery, is a lesbian involved in a relationship with a very butch lover. The characters, especially the heart-wrenchingly sweet Polly, make this a special film experience. (This video is currently out of print and is not available for sale, but may possibly be found for rent.)

Isle of Lesbos (1996, 98 min, U.S.)
Director: Jeff B. Harmon   Studio: Indie-Underground
Starring: Kirsten Holly Smith, Danica Sheridan, Sonya Hensley,
Michael Dotson, Alex Boling, Janet Krajeski, Sabrina Lu,
Dionysius Burbano, Calvin Grant, Jeff B. Harmon
This high energy, patently offensive musical romp (think *The Wizard of Oz* meets *The Rocky Horror Picture Show* as staged by Busby Berkeley) will have you either dancing in the aisles or running for the exits. In Bumbuck, Arkansas, a dirt-water town peopled by white Bible-thumping hicks, we find Alice, a sweet young thing who, in a moment of despair before her shotgun wedding, kills herself. She reemerges on the Isle of Sapphos—an Amazonian underworld led by a corpulent queen (Blatz Balinski, a bear-guzzling bull-dyke) who rules over a bevy of gorgeous, scantily clad lesbian subjects. Alice discovers her sexual wonderland as she embraces the Sapphic way of life. But the folks from back home arrive determined to take her back to their heterosexual world.

Le Jupon Rouge (1987, 90 min, France)
Director: Geneviève Lefèbvre   Studio: Strand Releasing
Starring: Marie-Christine Barrault, Alida Valli,
Guillemette Groban

Three women of greatly differing ages and backgrounds engage in a complicated relationship with one another. Manuela (Marie-Christine Barrault) has a nominal relationship with her boyfriend, but is actually more committed to her political work. She meets an older woman, Bacha (Alida Valli), a holocaust survivor and activist, and the two strike up a friendship, which becomes strained when Manuela begins a passionate love affair with another woman. (French with subtitles)

Just the Two of Us (1970, 82 min, U.S.)
Director: Barbara Peters   Studio: Something Weird
Starring: Alicia Courtney, Elizabeth Plumb
Pretty and sensible Denise (Alicia Courtney) and the sweetly ditsy blonde Adria (Elizabeth Plumb) are lonely housewives living in suburban L.A. who become close friends. While lunching at a restaurant, they notice two women at another table kissing. Both women are transfixed, and a romance between them ensues. However, what is a fling to one becomes much more to the other.

Late Bloomers (1997, 104 min, U.S.)
Director: Gretchen Dyer & Julia Dyer   Studio: Strand Releasing
Starring: Connie Nelson, Dee Hennigan, Gary Carter,
Lisa Peterson, Val Lumpkin
This comedy-drama is set in Eleanor Roosevelt High School where Dinah, a gangly math teacher and basketball coach, becomes friends with the cute but doughy Carly, a married school secretary and mother of two. What begins as innocent friendship soon becomes much more. As the two become more bold in their public affection for each other, Carly's husband, her sensitive daughter and young son, as well as neighbors and coworkers, begin to talk and become increasingly troubled. But romance triumphs over all adversities as the two women throw caution to the wind and fall passionately in love with each other.

Lianna (1982, 110 min, U.S.)

Director: John Sayles   Studio: Winwood Company
Starring: Linda Griffiths, Jane Hallaren, Jon DeVries

Director-writer Sayles' exceptional and humorous exploration of the coming out of the "good wife" offers a compassionate view of lesbianism, self-determination, and unrest. Lianna (Linda Griffiths) confronts her husband's infidelity, falls in love with her female graduate instructor, and sets out on her own. Sayles directs with a sensitive hand, and his perceptive screenplay contains many vulnerable and tender moments examining one woman's budding lesbian self-realization. (This video is currently out of print and is not available for sale, but may possibly be found for rent.)

Maedchen in Uniform (1931, 89 min, Germany)

Director: Leontine Sagan   Studio: Home Vision
Starring: Hertha Thiele, Dorothea Wieck

Written by lesbian poet Christa Winsloe and based on her play *Yesterday and Today,* this landmark film revolves around a young girl who is sent to a repressive Prussian boarding school where she develops an "unnatural" attachment to her female teacher. While the headmistress declares Manuela's affections to be scandalous, her classmates convey their support and understanding. (German with subtitles)

Oranges Are Not the Only Fruit (1989, 165 min, GB)

Director: Beeban Kidron   Studio: Fox/BBC
Starring: Geraldine McEwan, Charlotte Coleman

Adapted for BBC-TV by Jeanette Winterson from her novel of the same name, *Oranges* chronicles the coming-of-age of a young British lesbian, Jess (Geraldine McEwanin). In her turbulent struggles with her domineering evangelist mother (Charlotte Coleman), Jess grows up to be a fiercely independent young woman. (This video is currently out of print and is not available for sale, but may possibly be found for rent.)

Orlando (1993, 93 min, GB)
Director: Sally Porter   Studio: Columbia
Starring: Tilda Swinton, Billy Zane, Quentin Crisp,
Lothaire Bluteau, John Wood, Jimmy Somerville

This sumptuously filmed comedy of sexual mores, attitudes, and gender-switching stars the luminous Tilda Swinton as Orlando, a bewitchingly androgynous young man in the 1600s who, through a deal made with Queen Elizabeth I (regally played by Quentin Crisp), becomes immortal. As the centuries go by, Orlando strolls through the elaborate pageant that is English history, and during his adventures for love and self-discovery, he changes sexes, yet all the while, retaining his/her independence, kind heart, and a droll sense of humor about her adventure-filled fate. Though this film is not overtly lesbian, it was adapted from Virginia Woolf's novel of the same name, which was written for her lesbian lover.

Pandora's Box (1928, 110 min, Germany)
Director: G.W. Pabst   Studio: Kino
Starring: Louise Brooks, Fritz Kortner

This expressionistic classic features a luminous Louise Brooks as the sexually insatiable Lulu, a prostitute who ensnares a series of men and one woman with her fetching beauty and beguiling indifference. This is the first film to present a well-developed lesbian character, Countess Geschwitz (Alice Roberts), one of the people who falls in love with the temptress.

Paris Was a Woman (1995, 75 min, U.S.)
Director: Greta Schiller   Studio: Zeitgeist
Starring: Sharl Benstock, Berthe Cleyrergue, Giselle Freund,
Sam Steward, Dr. Catherine Stimpson

From the director of *Before Stonewall* comes this alternately interesting and scholarly documentary centering on the lives of several expatriates who lived and worked in Paris between the wars. Paris, specifically the area known as the Left Bank, became an intellectual, religious, racial, sexual, and political haven for so many artists, including Hemingway, Joyce, and Picasso. But this well-researched documentary probes past the era's "stars" and focuses on the many women and lesbians who also thrived there: Gertrude Stein and Alice Toklas, publishers Sylvia Beach and Adrienne Monnier, *New Yorker* columnist Janet Flanner, heiress Natalie Barney, painter Romaine Brooks, and Djuna Barnes and her lover Thelma Woods.

Personal Best (1982, 124 min, U.S.)

Director: Robert Towne   Studio: Warner
Starring: Mariel Hemingway, Patrice Donnelly, Scott Glenn

One of the earliest and best handled Hollywood dramas on lesbianism. The story follows the relationship of two women athletes who become friends and then lovers during tryouts for the Olympics. Mariel Hemingway is tenderly affecting as the younger, inexperienced woman who finds that her love for this woman is a fleeting foray on the road to her eventual heterosexual life.

Queen Christina (1933, 97 min, U.S.)

Director: Rouben Mamoulian
Starring: Greta Garbo, John Gilbert, Lewis Stone

This classic drama features a severely beautiful Greta Garbo as the reluctant queen who spends much of the film dressed as a male. In an early scene, a trouser-wearing Garbo hugs and plants a full kiss on her lady-in-waiting (Elizabeth Young). Later, Christina comes upon the woman pledging her love to a man; jealous and hurt, she impetuously runs away from the castle. Christina eventually falls in love with a Spanish emissary, and the drama quickly turns into a heterosexual love story.

The Rainbow (1989, 104 min, GB)

Director: Ken Russell   Studio: Vestron Pictures
Starring: Sammi Davis, Amanda Donohoe, Glenda Jackson,
Christopher Gable

Sammi Davis is great as Ursula, the earnest young woman whose sexuality erupts as she yearns for true love, self-respect, and independence in a society which frowns on all three. Amanda Donohoe is delightfully decadent as Winifred, Ursula's gym instructor, seductress, and mentor. (This video is currently out of print and is not available for sale, but may possibly be found for rent.)

Salmonberries (1991, 94 min, U.S.)

Director: Percy Adlon   Studio: Wolfe
Starring: k.d. lang, Rosel Zech

Lesbian song goddess k.d. lang bares her soul in this Canadian love story from the director of *Bagdad Cafe*. Not exactly a fulfilling experience for lesbians (no consummation), it is the presence of lang and her accomplished soundtrack that makes the film notable.

Seduction: The Cruel Woman (1985, 84 min, Germany)

Director: Monica Treut (& Elfie Mikesch)
Studio: First Run Features
Starring: Mechthild Grossmann, Sheila McLaughlin

This highly stylized and dreamlike exploration of sadomasochism stars Mechthild Grossmann as Wanda, a glamorous dominatrix and proprietor of the local "gallery" of bondage. As she moves from lesbian relationship to relationship, the film plumbs the depths of the dark side of sexual desire. Sheila McLaughlin also stars in this slick visual fantasy, which is inspired as much by the photography of Helmut Newton as by Leopold Sacher-Masoch's 1869 work *Venus in Furs*. (German with subtitles)

Serving in Silence—The Margarethe Cammermeyer Story (1995, 100 min, U.S.)

Director: Jeff Bleckner   Studio: Columbia
Starring: Glenn Close, Judy Davis, Jan Rubés,
Wendy Makkena, Margarethe Cammermeyer

This is a television dramatization of the true story of Colonel Margarethe Cammermeyer's battle to remain in the army after she came out as a lesbian. The Barbra Streisand-produced story stars Glenn Close as the 26-year veteran Bronze Star winner and former Nurse of the Year who was booted out of the armed forces when, during routine security clearance screening, she admitted to being a lesbian. Close is steadfastly determined (and a bit cold) as a woman who refuses to compromise her beliefs and resolutely seeks reinstatement through the legal system despite pressure from the army, her children, her former husband, and even her artist lover (played by Judy Davis).

The Sex Monster (1999, 97 min, U.S.)

Director: Mike Binder   Studio: Trimark
Starring: Mike Binder, Mariel Hemingway, Renée Humphrey,
Taylor Nichols, Missy Crider, Christopher Lawford,
Joanna Heimbold, Kevin Pollak, Stephen Baldwin

This sex comedy centers on the premise: What if you convinced your wife to have a ménage-a-trois and she liked it so much you find yourself sleeping on the couch? Mariel Hemingway stars as a quietly contented wife, Laura, whose libido is set afire after she reluctantly agrees to allow another women in bed with her and her husband. Laura's long pent-up lesbian desires explode into a frenzy of kisses, grinding, and other oral pleasuring, and all of this action leaves poor Marty the odd man out.

She Must Be Seeing Things (1988, 85 min, U.S.)

Director: Sheila McLaughlin   Studio: First Run Features
Starring: Sheila Dabney, Lois Weaver

This interesting love story follows the rocky relationship of Agatha, a New York lawyer, and Jo, a filmmaker. While Jo is out of town, Agatha comes upon her diary and photos, which suggest that she is developing an interest in men and may be unfaithful to her. Agatha's growing jealousy and her frantic attempts to keep her wavering lover interested result in her donning men's clothing and spying on her unsuspecting partner.

Show Me Love (1998, 89 min, Sweden)
Director: Lukas Moodysson   Studio: Strand Releasing
Starring: Alexandra Dahlstrom, Rebecca Liljeberg, Erica Carlson, Mathias Rust, Stefan Horberg, Josefin Nyberg
This comedic, romantic Swedish drama is set in the backwater town Amal and follows teenager Agnes (Liljeberg), a serious, dark-haired high school outsider who secretly falls in love with the carefree Elin (Dahlstrom), one of the cool "in" girls. Agnes is a troubled baby dyke who needs a hand. How Elin reaches out to the other teen and how their friendship turns to a relationship is told in a sympathetic, uplifting, and wonderfully romantic fashion. (Swedish with English subtitles)

Therese and Isabelle (1968, 102 min, France)
Director: Radley Metzger   Studio: First Run//Image
Starring: Essy Persson, Anna Gael, Barbara Laage, Anne Vernon
Set in an all-girls' Catholic boarding school, this milestone film is a tender glimpse at the erotic affair of two young women. Unlike many other works of the period, this provocative drama offers a non-exploitative picture of budding female sexuality, some very hot love scenes, and lots of schoolgirl emotional tension. (French with English subtitles)

Thin Ice (1995, 88 min, GB)
Director: Fiona Cunningham Reid   Studio: Wolfe
Starring: Sabra Willams, Charlotte Avery

When black photographer and amateur skater (Williams) loses her bed and skating partner shortly before competing in the 1994 Gay Games, she begins a desperate search for a suitable replacement. She thinks she finds one in Nathalie (Avery), a young "straight" woman and skating novice. While the two fine-tune their technique on the ice, they also begin a romance that proves to be just as difficult to master. A heart-warming romantic comedy.

Three of Hearts (1993, 101 min, U.S.)

Director: Yurek Bogayevicz   Studio: Turner
Starring: Sherilyn Fenn, Kelly Lynch,
William Baldwin, Joe Pantoliano

Stung by her sudden breakup with Ellen (Sherilyn Fenn), the lovelorn Connie (Kelly Lynch) concocts a wild plan for reconciliation. She hires male hustler Joey (William Baldwin) to seduce and abandon Ellen, breaking her heart so Connie can get her back on the rebound. Though not the breakthrough Hollywood lesbian film it promised to be, veering into the comforting embrace of heterosexuality, it is still remarkably charming and far from a complete failure in dealing with lesbian issues.

The Virgin Machine (1988, 85 min, Germany)

Director: Monika Treut   Studio: First Run Features
Starring: Ina Blum, Susie Bright

This thought-provoking sexual odyssey tells the story of a young West German woman and her search for "romantic love." Frustrated by the emptiness of her native Hamburg, Dorothee decides to flee her home to search for her mother, who is living in San Francisco. Once arrived, however, her trek turns into a process of sexual discovery. Filmed in a steamy black and white, the film exudes a sensuality in which simple lust is transformed into glorious eroticism. (English and German with English subtitles)

A Woman Like Eve (1979, 100 min, Netherlands)

Director: Noichka van Brakel   Studio: Sigma Film Productions
Starring: Maria Schneider, Monique Van De Ven

This sensitive drama stars Monique Van De Ven as Eve, whose secure but unhappy marriage ends in divorce when she finds fulfillment in the arms of a free-spirited lesbian folk singer played by Maria Schneider. An early European effort at a positive portrayal of lesbians, which was made by a production crew made up primarily of women. (This video is currently out of print and is not available for sale, but may be found for rent.)

When Night Is Falling (1994, 96 min, Canada)

Director: Patricia Rozema   Studio: Wolfe
Starring: Pascale Bussières, Rachael Crawford, Henry Czerny

Camille (Pascale Bussières) is a Christian academician romantically involved with Martin (Henry Czerny), a nice enough fellow teacher more interested in advancement than romance. Camille's repressed emotions and desire for true love come to the surface after she meets flamboyant circus performer Petra (Rachael Crawford). Despite being opposites, the two are attracted to each other. Initially denying her sexual attraction to the exotic African-Canadian Petra, Camille plays a repetitive game of "I want you, no, I don't"; that is, until Camille finally unleashes her pent-up desires in one of the more sexually charged lesbian love scenes ever filmed.

Wild Side (1995, 96 min, U.S.)

Director: Franklin Brauner   Studio: Pioneer
Starring: Christopher Walken, Anne Heche,
Steven Bauer, Joan Chen

This torrid love story is packaged in the guise of a standard straight-to-video soft-core action/thriller. Anne Heche is Alex Lee, a banker by day and a high-class hooker by night. Both of her careers are sent into a tailspin after a $1,500 tryst with Bruno Buckingham

(Christopher Walken), a bug-eyed, high-living businessman with criminal intentions. An elegant and gorgeous Joan Chen is Virginia Chow, Bruno's wife, who meets and immediately is attracted to the beautiful Alex. Before she realizes it, Alex is caught up in a plot to inject a computer virus into the national banking system, is a pawn of a sex-crazed FBI man, and in love (with Virginia) for the first time. This is an action/thriller that is actually a lesbian wet dream in disguise.

All these lesbian films, and more, are listed with direct live links to TLA's great site at:

www.amazingdreampublishing.com/filmreviews.html

CHAPTER 10

Counseling from a therapist's point of view

Introduction

Since many people are unfamiliar with counseling, I have prepared this chapter to help you know what to expect if you choose to work with a counselor or therapist. Included are facts on what both the American Psychiatric Association and the American Psychological Association term lesbians and gay men, and information from research I've done regarding lesbians' and gay men's counseling issues.   —*K.W.*

What do the mental health associations say about lesbians?

It has been estimated that one in ten individuals is gay or lesbian. That means that out of one million people, at least 100,000 are gay. Other sources say two in ten is a more accurate depiction of our numbers. Whatever percentage is correct, it shows that there are millions of gay people who are making contributions to societies around the world.

In 1973, the American Psychiatric Association declared that homosexuality was no longer considered a mental illness, and in 1975 the American Psychological Association followed suit.

Research concerning twins has shown there may be a genetic component, but not in all cases, and studies of the brain have shown some slight differences between gay and straight men. There is still no conclusive evidence on what causes sexual orientation. More and more it is thought to have a genetic component, and the fact remains that there have been gay people throughout history.

Your options for counseling

You may go to a private therapist or a community mental health center. There are many pros and cons to both depending upon your needs. If you work during the day, evening appointments fit better with your schedule. Some private therapists offer this service, but most agencies do not. If you are interested in or have been recommended to use group therapy, community mental health centers have this option, while private therapists may or may not run groups.

Finding and setting up an appointment with a private therapist

If you choose to see a private therapist, I suggest that you ask people you know if they could recommend someone. If you don't feel comfortable asking friends, private therapists are sometimes listed in your local lesbian/gay paper.

When you decide on a therapist, you need to contact their office to see if they are accepting new clients, or if there is a long waiting period before you can set up an appointment. If they are accepting new clients, you can ask to interview your prospective new therapist to see if you feel comfortable. A counseling relationship is like any other relationship—you're either going to click with the person or you're not. It's better to get a feel for a therapist before you decide to schedule an appointment with her, and you can do this by phone.

During the interview, you can ask questions about her style of counseling such as: does she follow a specific counseling theory, and how does this theory work? What would a typical session be like? Tell her your reason to begin therapy, and ask if she is comfortable with sexual orientation issues if you don't know she is lesbian-friendly. Find out how she will work with you. I would suggest interviewing several private therapists. If you have insurance that covers therapy, ask if she is a provider of your insurance company.

Check with your insurance company, or human resources office, to verify exactly what your counseling benefits cover. Some insurance companies send people to EAP (employee assistance programs). These programs are usually limited to three to six sessions. With EAP programs you are often assigned to a therapist. If the first interview with an EAP therapist determines an issue will take more than three to six sessions, you will most likely be referred to a private therapist who is authorized for reimbursement by your insurance company. If you are referred out, they will either contact the therapist for you or give you the names and numbers so that you can arrange your own appointment. Ask for two to three names so you can interview the EAP providers. Once you settle on a therapist, schedule an appointment for your first session. Depending on your symptoms or issues, the therapist may suggest you consider medication and refer you to a psychiatrist. Some private therapists work alone while others may be in a group practice that includes a psychiatrist.

Community mental health centers

If you choose to go to a community mental health center, call for an initial appointment. The support staff may or may not ask you the reason you need to see a therapist. If they ask be honest. Your answer may determine with whom your initial counseling appointment will be. If they set up an appointment with a therapist when you call, you should advise them of any preferences you may have concerning your therapist, such as male or female. If they are able, the support staff will try to accommodate your request.

You may be asked to come in and fill out demographic paperwork before you are scheduled to see your new therapist. You will need to disclose basic information about yourself, such as your home address and phone number; information on your employment and health insurance company (if you have health insurance, they will need your card); social security number; basic health information; and why you are seeking counseling. After filling out your paperwork, you may see a therapist for an intake or you may have to schedule an intake appointment.

The intake will involve you and the therapist evaluating what services the mental health center has that you would benefit from, and if you should consider medication if your symptoms indicate to the therapist that there may be a need. An appointment will then be scheduled for you to meet with a psychiatrist who will be able to write your prescription.

Fees

If you receive services at a community mental health center, the agency has hired your therapist to provide counseling services to you. These services are usually billed per hour. They can be billed as a full fee or on a sliding scale based on your household income. If you have health insurance, it may or may not pay for all or a portion of your appointments. Check your policy before you go to the mental health facility The support staff should meet with you to determine the cost of the services you will receive and if they accept payment from your insurance company.

There are usually separate charges for individual therapy, group therapy, and appointments with a psychiatrist. The person meeting with you should provide a breakdown of each of these categories. If the cost set for you is beyond your means to pay, let the center know immediately. Sometimes there are procedures in place wherein the center may appeal for a reduction in the cost of the services you will receive, or they may offer to work out a payment plan.

A private therapist may also work on a sliding scale or be willing to work out a payment plan if you do not have insurance coverage, or if the private therapist is not covered by your EAP or insurance company. If you find a therapist you like who is not covered by your insurance, ask about payment options.

Your intake session with a private or community mental health therapist

The first meeting with a therapist will be to review what brings you in, your history, family history, sexual abuse history (if any), and any problems you may have, or have had, with self-harm (suicidality) or harm toward others (homicidality). There may be more questions depending on the therapist, the agency, or the state you reside in. Different states will require agencies to gather some information that others may not. The gathering of your personal information is called an intake.

The therapist will most likely review with you how the issue you are wanting to deal with is affecting your life, and the two of you will set up the goal(s) of your sessions. Goals are sometimes revised as your sessions continue. Remember, in any counseling session, if you don't understand something your therapist says or why she says it, you have the right to ask about it. You also have the right to open a discussion if you don't agree with something the therapist says.

Many therapists will give homework assignments. These are designed to help you continue the work you are doing during your sessions or to expand upon it. These assignments could be to read a specific book (bibliotherapy); to journal, which means keeping track of your thoughts and feelings each day, or what you think and feel about specific issues your therapist assigns to you to write about; or to practice a certain behavior(s). There may also be deep breathing exercises and other assignments that are too numerous to describe. The assignments listed above are some of the more common ones.

The counseling process

I see therapy as a cooperative effort between the therapist and the client. Progress depends on many things including motivation, effort, and other life circumstances such as your interactions with family, friends, and associates. The goals, methods, and treatment should be agreed upon by all involved. These factors may determine the pace of your progress as well as your results. In all settings it is required that clients are given a diagnosis which will become a part of your confidential record. This is because of a combination of state requirements and insurance company requirements.

Your first session

When you have your first session, the therapist will probably discuss your situation and work with you to determine general goals. Like any new relationship, there may be a bit of apprehension or you may feel nervous during your first session. Let the therapist know you are nervous so that she can work with you. After the first few sessions, if you feel there is a personality conflict discuss this with your therapist. See if you can work out any differences. If you and the therapist feel good about the results, you can continue with counseling. If you aren't comfortable, then you can consider finding another therapist. Remember, you are the one who decided to seek help, and you always have the choice to change your mind about who you want to accompany you on your journey.

If you want a family member(s) or significant other to join you in a session, discuss this with your therapist in advance. She will know what you wish to work on in the session, and will probably discuss if this would be constructive for your progress at that point in your treatment.

Some methods used in therapy

There are numerous ways to help someone who is having difficulties such as: relaxation techniques, conflict management, learning effective communication skills, behavioral contracts, and positive self-talk. Your therapist will be happy to answer any questions you may have about therapeutic approaches. Depending on your issues, you may be encouraged to join a group (either treatment or support/self-help such as AA, NA, etc.) or have one-on-one sessions.

Group sessions usually involve five or more people who are experiencing similar situations. One or two therapists may facilitate the sessions, which can deal with depression, emotion regulation, management of symptoms, or coping skills, to name a few. In many cases, group therapy can be a very positive experience. Hearing other people's experiences can help you to understand you're not alone, get support from others who have experienced similar things, and get feedback from others who are supportive and caring concerning your situation.

One-on-one sessions are approximately fifty minutes and involve just you and your therapist. Sometimes the therapist may take notes to focus on key issues. This is so she can review your progress. Session frequency is worked out between you and your therapist.

If you are in an emergency situation, call your therapist. Let her know this is a crisis and how to reach you. After you leave the message and where to call, stay off the phone and stay at home. You'd be surprised how many people will leave a message, then leave home, or get on the phone. Also, keep in mind that your therapist is seeing clients and is usually only free for about ten minutes between each appointment. She will get back to you as soon as she can. If a client does not show up for an appointment, your therapist can possibly spend more than ten minutes with you on the phone.

Sometimes matters get worse before they get better. For example, during the counseling process you may experience feelings such as intense sadness, frustration, anxiety, or guilt. You may find that some relationships become more difficult due to the changes you're making. These experiences are not uncommon and can be surpassed with continued work with your therapist.

Confidentiality

All the information you share with your therapist, and all of your records are confidential. That means that your therapist will not communicate information concerning you and your treatment to any other individual. Your diagnosis, treatment status, or history will not be revealed without a Release of Information form signed by you. Only under special circumstances can a therapist not guarantee confidentiality:

1. If you (and/or your family member or partner) communicate a threat to harm another person

2. If you (and/or your family member or partner) threaten to harm yourself or are unable to care for yourself

3. If your therapist suspects abuse or neglect of a child, helpless adult or an elder, then federal laws mandate your therapist break confidentiality.

Considerations

If you have to cancel an appointment, make sure to call at least twenty-four hours in advance if possible. This will help your therapist schedule someone else for your session who may need it. Also, some agencies will charge you if you do not abide by their cancellation policies, so make sure to ask about the correct procedure during your first visit

If your purpose for seeing a therapist is couples counseling or family counseling, this should be the focus in your sessions. You and your partner, or family members, should not be seeing the same therapist for individual therapy. If a therapist sees you and your partner, or family members, individually this can cause a conflict of interest and possibly lead to your confidentiality being broken. This is not to say that you can't see a therapist for individual issues and occasionally ask for your partner, or your family, to join your sessions to work on specific issues.

Handling complaints

Anytime you find yourself dissatisfied with the counseling process, do not be afraid or intimidated to let your counselor know immediately. She will be willing to work out any difficulties that may arise. If you are unable to resolve the issue then the following options can be explored:

1. Transfer to another therapist. If you are involved with a group practice or community mental health setting you can do so within the agency.

2. You may contact the counselor's supervisor if she or he has one.

If you feel that you have been treated unethically and cannot resolve the issue with your therapist or her/his supervisor, then you may decide to contact the State Board that regulates the licensure of your therapist. There are several licenses: L.C.S.W. (licensed clinical social worker), L.P.C. (licensed professional counselor), L.M.F.T. (licensed marriage and family therapist), Psy.D. (clinical psychologist), Ph.D. (psychologist), and M.D. (Psychiatrist).

Through the looking glass: A section for therapists unfamiliar with lesbians and gays

The current literature is in agreement that homosexuality is not learned. It is commonly understood that those who are lesbian or gay are born that way. Some know all of their lives that they are homosexual, while others do not come to terms with their sexuality until later in life. Growing up is difficult for gay people. As a child there are messages from society that say it is wrong to be gay. We are still bombarded with stereotypical examples of effeminate men and masculine women. There are few positive role models for gay people, let alone children who are gay. Many gay people state that they realized they were "different" at adolescence and sometimes earlier, and some report that they were already adults when they realized their attraction for others of the same sex.

It is important to realize that not all lesbians are masculine in appearance, and that not all gay men are effeminate. Those who are "stereotypical" do not make up the entire population of gay communities. It is also important to note that lesbians do not want to be men and that gay men do not want to be women. They are simply individuals who are attracted to others of the same sex for fulfillment of affectional and sexual needs.

We have all heard the terms "dyke," "faggot," "queer," and "fairy." These terms are full of anger and intolerance. They are words that are used to hurt and demean others and to ease the fear of someone who does not understand. Society has given us the lesson that to be gay is to be an object of contempt. There is pain in being an outcast because of homophobia; therefore, some lesbians and gay men hide this aspect of themselves.

A big problem that faces gay people who are hiding their

sexuality is low self-image. This is understandable when taking into account the views of society and how they are internalized. There are two coping strategies that can help in dealing with the low self-image: self-labeling as a lesbian and self-disclosure of sexual orientation to people who are supportive. These two strategies help the person to develop a positive homosexual identity. It is somewhat easier to come out now than it was in the past, but there is still the fear that a gay person's friends or family might reject them, or they might lose their employment or housing.

It is important to recognize and understand, from an ethical and humane standpoint, how therapists must acquaint themselves with community resources for their gay clients. Counselors should be sensitive to their gay clients' needs in order to help them cope with a society which mostly ostracizes them.

Here are a few of the issues which gay people can face:

1. Gay individuals can be victims of discrimination and prejudice. This includes negativity directed at a gay person, stereotyping, lack of support from peers, and discrimination in both housing and employment.

2. Dealing with family members is sometimes quite difficult. Even if a person has been honest and loving with her family her whole life, she may have problems sharing her sexuality with her parents. Common reasons for a person's silence may be fear of hurting or disappointing her parents or receiving negative reactions from them.

3. Gay clients need help with communication skills and development of a positive self-image. Substance abuse is one way gay people may learn to cope in a negative way. Also needed is a knowledge of relationship building

skills, especially since society does not provide nurturance for or acknowledgment of gay relationships, including monogamous lesbian or gay partnerships which may have lasted for decades. Gay partners who seek couples counseling should be able to focus on their relationship issues rather than problems stemming from being gay in today's world.

When surveyed most therapists agree that homosexuality is not a mental illness and that gays can be as well-adjusted as heterosexuals. Many feel gays should be able to adopt children if they are "fit" parents.

It is very important for heterosexual counselors to ethically meet the needs of their gay clients by educating themselves to the terminology used, understanding that the client was born gay and that it is an orientation that cannot be changed, and to make an effort to understand that their clients have no desire to be the opposite sex. It is also important to understand that gay individuals need to deal with problems of self-esteem due to the stress and pressure our society exerts to conform to a "heterosexual norm." Such understanding may be gained by continuing education workshops, research of current literature in the field, becoming familiar with resources within the community, and becoming clear about one's own feelings toward gay women and men. If a counselor or therapist is uncomfortable with a client who is a gay person, then ethically she/he must refer the client to another therapist.

CHAPTER 11

Coping with the world as a lesbian

The hard knocks

Being lesbian can be challenging sometimes, but we do have it way better than many in our past. Acceptance of lesbians in society has come a long way in the last twenty years, but it still has miles to go before we are treated equally with other tax-paying citizens of the U.S.A. When you are young it is even harder. Employers sometimes use your energy to benefit themselves, and this can result in lousy pay and possibly low self-esteem. The only thing I know to do is to always be the best person you can be. Keep your dreams firmly in your mind, pick your battles wisely, but don't put up with too much crap.

Things I've learned as a lesbian so far

The following pages contain mottos I've used during my time on earth. As with the rest of the commentary in this book, these are my opinions stemming from some hard lessons I've chosen to improve who I am. They may or may not help you in dealing with life as a lesbian, but they might give you a good start in finding your own path.

Everyone is born with gifts. It doesn't matter what that gift might be, it is yours alone. It is up to you to utilize it and make it into something successful in your life. Whether it's being a great cook, mom, or musician, don't let your gift go to waste. If you don't know what your gift is, do things you like until you figure it out. Take art, music, or writing classes; learn how to use a computer; train your dog how to shake or your cat how to fetch; draw huge love letters in the sand on a beach; sit by a lake and watch the clouds. Remember your childhood dreams of what you wanted to be when you grew up, and see if they still make you smile. Somewhere in your life is the clue of who you are and what you are meant to become, so be a great detective and find out what it is.

Love the planet. Look at nature with new eyes. After all, the earth is our mother—the one who covers us with beautiful skies and nighttime galaxies. Without her, our bodies would only be stardust floating in the universe. She's way older than we are, so respect your elder.

There's a lot of pollution going on right now, and millions of acres of rain forests are being destroyed, which cuts the oxygen and kills thousands of plant and animal species we may never see again. There's a hole in the earth's aura, the ozone layer, and huge gaping cavities under her skin from our bloodletting of oil and explosions during nuclear testing. All this abuse could end in the earth eventually retaliating, so do what you can. Doing something good for the earth is doing something good for yourself. Recycle everything possible, don't litter, and send lots of love and energy her way by enjoying the natural beauty. Love your life here. It's just a breath in the range of infinity.

You don't have to go along with the crowd. If you don't agree with what is going on around you, use your right as a free human being and vacate the premises. Only your soul knows what is right for you. Don't ever let anyone make those kinds of decisions that could affect your freedom or your future.

Limit drinking, smoking, and drugging. Anything can become a habit, and anything done to excess can be detrimental to your life on earth. Chemical dependencies steal your energy and make it harder to stay grounded. If you are drunk or high, you sure can't defend yourself, and you sure can't make good decisions either. If you don't want to drink or do drugs, stand your ground. If people tease you at parties and ask "If you don't drink or smoke, what do you do?" just smile and say "I have spectacular sex!" I've used this exact answer many times, and I've had very good results. The gaping-mouthed partygoers don't usually ask again.

Everyone has her own path. Just because you don't agree with what someone is doing doesn't mean it is not right for that person. If she asks you for advice, give it in a loving way, but don't be mad if she doesn't take it. We all have our own lessons to learn, and sometimes people need a few hard knocks to learn something. The best thing to do is stand back and let other folks do what they need to do. If it starts making you crazy then maybe you should not be involved with them, or maybe you are seeing things within them that you don't like in yourself. Remember, everyone is like a mirror. If you don't like the reflection you are seeing then change yourself, because you sure aren't going to change them.

Don't judge other people. This is an oldy but a goody, and sometimes it is hard to do. When the feelings of judgment start to come up, and I think it is pretty normal for most human beings to have moments of this, then reread the passage above concerning everyone having a path. That should help to put judgment in perspective a bit.

The finger-pointing routine. This is similar to the judging section except a little more vile. Sometimes people do this to divert attention from themselves or their situation. I had this happen in the worst way when I was raising my stepdaughter with my ex. Another student at her junior high was also being raised by a lesbian couple, and when the issue came up she immediately pointed her finger at my stepdaughter. The kids started harassing her, calling her fag and lez. The result of this incident went on for two years until my step-daughter finally quit the eleventh grade and enrolled in night school.

When people start pointing a finger at another, accusing them of whatever, there are three fingers pointing right back at themselves. The old Shakespearean passage "I think she doth protest too much" rings true to this day. When anybody starts pointing the accusing finger, she better take a good hard look at herself in the mirror.

If you don't have anything good to say, then don't open your mouth. Now this is another old adage, but it is one that I live by and has many times saved my butt from huge problems. It is a true fact that many people love to stir up trouble. These people are looking for conflict and would love nothing more than to have you be right in the middle of a fight that they can watch and gossip about. Why let them have fun at your expense? Watch what you say and who you say it to, especially in the workplace, and remember a closed mouth gathers no feet.

If someone is treating you unfairly, change your situation. This can happen anywhere and to anyone. I've found that at the core of the problem, when it happens to me, is usually my own self-worth. If you had a rough childhood, this dilemma can be even worse. It is a struggle to realize and truly know that you are a special person who is meant to be here on the earth at this very moment. Even if you don't believe in a higher power, the odds of you being conceived and born are huge, which makes you remarkable no matter what. If you find that you are in a bad situation, get out of it as soon as possible. If it is a problem job, find a new and better one. If it is a strained relationship with family, learn how to set limits in therapy and start doing it. The same if it is a partner. Life is just too short for us to let others sap our energy. Gather supportive friends around you, make a decision to change, and find a way out. Once the decision has been made in your heart, the doors will open, and things will be brighter soon.

Dream big. Don't sell yourself short. If you have a dream, keep at it until it manifests. Surround yourself with people who believe in you, and don't listen to the ones who say you won't make it. Many people want to drag down others who have dreams. It only results in pain, frustration, and anger if you listen to their opinion of what you should be or do. They don't know your heart, your strength, or the sheer power of your will. Make it a point to prove them wrong.

The best revenge is success. Now some people will take offense at the wording of this, but it is one of my favorites. People in my past would have been happier than hogs in slop to see me lying in the ditch of total defeat, but there is no way I would let that happen. Instead of getting even with the way they treated me, I decided not to stoop to their level. I turned that negative, pained energy into creativity, and I have never gone back since. If someone treats you badly, or discounts you for being who you are, don't allow them to take your power. Give yourself a little time for the hurt to heal, then go out and use your gifts for the betterment of yourself and everyone else. The world loves a winner, so take hold of your life and be one!

Whose life is it? Don't let others take over and run your adult life. If people start telling you what to do and how to do it, and generally being huge pains in the butt, simply advise them that since they want to run your life so badly, you expect them to house and clothe you, and that from now on you will be sending them all of your bills. If this doesn't work, vacate the relationship as fast as you can. Decide that your next friends, or partner, will treat you like an equal instead of a helpless child.

Whose loss is it? Asking myself this question helps me to feel better about handling certain situations. If I know in my heart that I have treated someone with the respect and dignity that every person deserves, but they still persist in treating me badly, then they may have a mental illness. In this case you must take that into account and do the best thing for yourself, which is change the circumstance. This may mean vacating the relationship. Don't expect them to change, but if you lower yourself to being as nasty as they are, it will only hurt you later down the road. If you have a clear conscience about how you handled a situation, then you are the one who can sleep at night. If you have any doubts, ask yourself the following questions: "Whose loss is it really? Did they lose the possibility of an honest and caring friendship, or did I lose the possibility of a deceitful, back-biting, no-win relationship?" When you break a bad situation down into a few simple questions, it makes the answer very obvious.You deserve better, so make a new choice for yourself.

People have a right to their own opinions. If you expect others to tolerate who you are as a lesbian, then you must tolerate them even if they are homophobic. Now, I don't mean go around and try to be their best friend or anything like that. What I do mean is negativity begets negativity. If you put out bad intentions they will come right back to you. The USA is supposedly a free country, which means people have a right to their own point of view. This includes religious beliefs, being racist, homophobic, or just a nasty ol' pig. I'm not saying these things are correct, but who am I to judge? It's not my right to be anyone's keeper but my own.

It's not good to shove your ideas down someone else's throat. This is similar to the passage above but a little different. There are many radical groups in the world, some who think that violence or death is the only way to get people's attention. In some circumstances retaliation works, like the gay uprising at Stonewall that set us all on the path to freedom, but what I'm really addressing here is small situations you may encounter on a daily basis.

Take an anti-fur demonstration I came upon one day. An older man had come out of a fur coat store and a small group of people outside started yelling at him and calling him murderer and killer among other things. He got so mad I thought he was going to have a heart attack, and I would bet money that the confrontation did not stop him from buying his wife a fur coat either. Now, maybe if these people would have given him a bit more dignity than accosting him on the street, he would have accepted their flyers showing the inhumane treatment of animals in the industry. I love animals and have ten of the furry creatures living in the same house with me, but standing next to this guy and hearing the abuse that was directed at him made me feel incredibly nervous and defensive, so much that I didn't hang around and listen to anything the protestors had to say.

I don't need that kind of abusive treatment in my life, and I sure won't tolerate it. I was always taught that you can catch more flies with honey than vinegar, and I've found it

165

is usually true. I'm not saying you should not speak your truth. I'm just saying there are better ways of doing it than screaming, threatening, and giving yourself and others around you a case of high blood pressure.

Don't be afraid to speak your mind. Now this was, and sometimes still is, a hard one for me to do. When you come from an abusive childhood, you may believe that what you think or feel does not matter. It took me years to learn how to speak my mind, and I have my partner to thank for it. Now I'm not saying you should just blurt out whatever is going on in your head, causing panic and chaos in everyone's life. What I am saying is that if you are having an issue about what someone said or did, think on it a while, sort out why it is bothering you, and if it is still an issue have a non-heated discussion. You will get used to doing this, and soon you will feel way better. Read that chapter on communication again if needed. It is one of the most important things you need to know as a human being.

Listening. Learning how to listen is just as important as speaking your mind. Sometimes if you are just learning how to communicate in a healthy manner, you may not be able to stop once you start. All those years of silence are finally free to flow out, and it's hard to rein that energy back in. You aren't learning much about how your partner feels or thinks when your own mouth is chattering nonstop. If this is a problem for you during an important discussion, each person should have a time allotment where the other does not interrupt them without permission. This is one way to learn how to listen.

Don't be afraid to love. This is a hard one sometimes, especially if you have been hurt in the past. If you hold back your love, you are only hurting yourself and your partner.

And if you don't have a partner, this may be the reason. Love is the only way to solve most of life's problems. You have to love the earth, the animals, and the people in order to figure out a way to make small changes that will help the injustices of the world. Holding back on emotions takes a lot of energy and weakens your body. Depending on the emotion, this can lead to illness. When you are lying on your death bed it will be too late to realize that you could have loved more and you could have done it better. Become a student of life. Treat yourself with love and respect, and others will do the same.

The dark night of the soul. Everyone has times when they feel like they've hit bottom. Sometimes we have to do this in order to clear out our expectations of what we thought life was supposed to be. The solution is usually giving your dilemma over to a higher power, and it's not always an easy thing to do. Whether it is your own power or the power of a Creator it really doesn't matter. When this happens to you, take time for yourself. Think about the path that you have been on, and ponder the idea that there may be another one filled with warm soft sand instead of cold sharp rocks. Find a close friend you can confide in, or if you are new to an area find a trusted counselor. Remember, it's always darkest before the dawn. Your life is precious and important. Do things that you love, like take hot sudsy baths, or go to the mountains and talk to the hummingbirds; listen to relaxing music, or read self-help books; whatever it takes, do it. You can get through this, and when you do you will be a much stronger person because of it.

Laugh as much as possible. Living today can be hard. Tragedies happen every moment, but they all occur for some reason, whether we know what it is or not. Fill your life with positive people who make you feel good about your gifts and who you are. Go to funny plays and movies, or watch your animals roughhouse in the yard. Limit your time viewing sad or violent dramas on TV or film. Find your favorite funny movie and buy a copy to watch when you are feeling blue. Laugh alone and the world may think you are a loon, but who cares?

Picking a partner. Do not settle for someone you can live with; only settle for someone that you cannot live without. You deserve the best, so go out and find her. Know in your heart that if it is meant to be, it will happen.

Hard lessons, mistakes, and total life screwups. Don't be ashamed of your mistakes. After all, experience is something you don't usually get until just after you need it. Everyone screws up, so don't let the memory of the situation haunt you and drag you down. Learn from your mistakes and make them your springboard for your next big accomplishment.

When someone insults you. This is always such an energy drain. Even though you might act as though the insult didn't hurt you, many times it lingers in your subconscious bringing up doubt when you may need strength. Most times, I've found that people who do this are either jealous of you for some reason, or they are just flat-out nasty and like to make others suffer so that they will feel better about themselves.

One time, out of the blue, an acquaintance of mine insulted my hair. Instead of me worrying about it I replied, "Gee Angela, I don't know if that was a compliment or not, but thanks anyway." She immediately stuck her foot in her mouth by saying "Well, it certainly wasn't a compliment!"

This made me laugh out loud, totally taking away the power of what she had said, and I am still laughing today. I didn't know until several years later that her girlfriend at the time had gone on and on about how much she loved my hair. So you can see how that whole situation went from Angela feeling threatened by her girlfriend's comment, into wanting to punish me for it. The question to ask is "Whose issue is it really?"

Jealousy, the worst enemy. To me the saddest thing anyone can be is jealous of someone else's accomplishments or situation. It zaps the energy right out of both people, sometimes making it impossible for either to use their gifts. Many times, jealousy is simply anger turned outward, like Angela in the previous passage. Other times it is the simple fact that one person would love to do what the other one is but feel they are not able. Maybe they are not seeing their own gifts, or maybe they are angry because they are too lazy to get off their own butt and do it for themselves.

When you see someone successful, most times they weren't just born that way. It takes hard work and devotion to your dreams to make a success in this world today. If you have jealous people in your life, talk to them about how hurtful it is. If they persist in the negativity, take leave of the relationship until something changes. It is their issue; don't allow it to become yours by not doing what you are supposed to in life, or holding yourself back. If you have issues with jealousy, work on finding your own gifts, not being envious of someone else's. No matter who you are or what you do, there will always be someone who can do it just a little better. Instead of making an enemy of her, make her your mentor. Nurture each other, because we are all on the path together.

Don't own other people's feelings. Just like opinions, people have a right to their own feelings. You cannot make them do or feel anything if they don't want to. If you are upset over something someone said or did to you, then you have three options: work through it on your own, which means resolving the pain you are feeling to a point of when you think of the issue it doesn't bother you anymore; stuff it, which means your body takes it on and you will still have painful emotions about it days, months, or even years later; or go and discuss it and find a resolution. You have to own your own actions and emotions. If you find out why something bothers you, it may not the next time it happens. This is called true healing.

Hate—a hateful word. This is a very strong word that I work very hard to keep out of my vocabulary. Sometimes hate is just fear stuffed way down deep inside of you. If you find yourself saying you hate something, take a look at why there is such a strong emotion attached to whatever it is. If someone says they hate you, they could be threatened by something you represent to them. Maybe you look like their oldest enemy who beat them up in grade school. Maybe they are so jealous of you that the emotion has turned into hate. Whatever it is, if someone hates you, it can become like a negative vortex that grows bigger and bigger as more people get involved.

When I was studying mechanical engineering in college, I had this happen to me. A young woman specializing in architectural engineering all of a sudden started glaring at me during breaks and saying that she hated me to other students. I had never even met her, but she persisted in being horribly nasty. Unbeknownst to me, I had been nominated for a state design achievement award and so had she. After one of my classmates came up and told me some of the things she had been saying, I finally had enough of it. I waited for her in the hall one day, and asked if I could speak to her in private. She was totally scared and tried to leave, but I kept calmly talking. I told her that I didn't know what I had done to offend her, and if she could please tell me I would do whatever I could to make up for it. Of course she couldn't say a word, and she was pretty embarrassed by her behavior. We didn't become grand old buddies, but the harassment from her totally stopped. I guess she had some jealousy that had turned into hatred. Whatever it was, it didn't work to her advantage, because I won the design award for that year.

Practice good manners. Smile at someone who seems to be feeling blue; open the door for the person you are with or for a stranger with her arms full; let someone who has only one item go ahead of you and your full cart at the grocery store; say thank you anytime anyone does something nice for you. These are a few of the ways you can practice being nice to your fellow human beings. Good manners are sometimes a rarity today. Everyone seems to be in such a big hurry to be first, they just forget what it is like to be polite. Treat other people the way you would like to be treated and see what happens.

Live in the present. This is one of the most important things to learn, and it can be kind of difficult to grasp at first. If you look at your life as a dotted line starting at your birth and ending when you leave this plane, then where you are now is just one dot on that line. Your body is right at that one dot—not on the dot behind it and not on the dot in front of it. Think of the dots as seconds of your life. What you are doing right now, this second, will never happen exactly the same again because it will be in the past.

The thing with being human is that we have a wonderful storehouse called our brain. It houses memories of everything we have ever seen, heard, touched, smelled, and tasted during our whole life. These memories sometimes have an emotion attached to them, and this is where the trouble can start. If you have had a bad experience and you do not let go of the emotion of it, it can haunt you later. Even though this experience may have happened years ago, that feeling can lock you into the past and keep you from growing now. The past is gone. If you find yourself dwelling on something that happened years ago, think about how it really cannot hurt you now unless you allow it. The same goes for worrying about the future that isn't even here yet. Only you can control your own thoughts.

If you find that you are constantly allowing the past or the future to hold you back, there is a little trick that helps. Think of the most pleasant situation that ever happened to you. It can be anything, from a beautiful sunset, to the way those chocolate chip cookies your loving grandmother fixed for you always smelled. For me it was the protected way I felt when I was with my horse. Find some memory that doesn't lead to any other feeling but peace and happiness; then name the memory something beautiful. When you feel the anxiety start to rise and the negative thought you've been dwelling on surface in your mind, immediately think of the name of your vision, and concentrate on seeing only that totally peaceful memory. It will take a few days to reprogram your mind but don't let up. This really worked for me, and I think it could work for you. Remember, all you truly have is this very moment. Make it the best it can be.

Patience. If you find yourself fuming at a traffic light or going into a road-rage fit behind a slowpoke, just think to yourself that this might be saving you from an accident or from receiving a ticket from that hidden police officer around the next bend. Look at the delays in life as meant to be. After all, it was your choice to go the way you did, so enjoy the trip.

The world owes no one a living. If you think you will be able to coast through life never doing anything to improve your situation, then you may die in a ditch. Even if you have wealthy parents, that money could float away if an investment goes bad or the fortune is mismanaged. Always have a backup plan, and be prepared to fend for yourself. You have to take care of you.

Higher education. No matter what a racket some educational institutions may be, to make a decent living in this world you pretty much have to have some kind of degree or certificate. Even if you are on your own and have little money, it pays to work towards a higher education. There are also plenty of scholarships, grants, and programs to help you do this. Go to your local technical school or community college, and speak to someone in the counseling department about work programs or other ways to go to their school. These people are paid to help you. Then, narrow down what you would like to study, research the career fields you could go into, and see if you could envision yourself doing this five days a week. Remember, a full-time job takes up almost a third of your life. Make it something you enjoy, and it will be more like play and less like work.

If something sounds too good to be true, it usually is. If you don't want to go to school right away, but you need a job it is real easy to get sucked into "get rich quick" schemes. Sometimes they are "investment loans," which means they will promise to turn the money into huge profits, which usually leads to you losing your investment when they leave town. The other more legitimate businesses will hire young people to get them more contacts. They will want you to sell their product to relatives and friends, which broadens their client base. Many of these products are really great, but usually the only person getting rich from selling them is the one above you, which leaves you struggling with a dead-end job. This happens a lot with selling merchandise in a pyramid sales technique.

Now I'm not saying you can't make a great living doing this. The person who will hire you is probably doing pretty well, but you can bet they had to work hard to get where they are in the company. What I am saying is that you have to have a certain type of personality to do this type of work. If your gift is to be an incredible sales person who could sell the spots right off of a dog, this may be your dream job. If you are not so hot at sales or not a savvy stock and investment person, steer clear of these rich dream promises. They may turn into nightmares that will steal your time or your money.

Money isn't everything. I know it helps to have money, but money doesn't mean you are a good person. I have known corrupt rich people, and I've also known poor people who were like saints on earth. I was taken in by a family like that when I was thrown out of my home at seventeen. What I am saying here is don't be swept away by someone just because they are rich. Money doesn't make a person honest or good-natured, and it sure doesn't have the power to make a sad, depressed person happy. It can be used for the good of others or for evil. Just look around you and see the little groups of people who hold themselves away from others because of money. If you have issues with money, read that book *Excuse Me, Your LIFE is Waiting.*

Look at the person inside instead of the body outside. Everyone's body is different. Some people are big-boned mammas who can belt out a song or a smile, and some are like thin mints who can dance like angels. Basically, I think our bodies are like shopping bags that we picked out to hold our souls for this life. Some of us chose sleek black jewelry bags and some of us chose huge white department store bags. Some of us chose paper and others chose plastic. The point is that these "bags" that are housing our true selves are not permanent. We only have a small time on this earth together, so instead of us fighting about our differences in taste or our choices for our lessons in this life, why don't we look at what's real. The truth of what we really are is always inside. We could be the most beautiful person in the world and still have a nasty disposition, or we could be the homeliest person and be an angel incarnate.

Do unto others. Another oldie but goody, this one goes a long way to making your life happier. If you really want the best for yourself, meaning honesty, love, and good friends, then put out those things to those around you. Learn to be the best person you can be by freely helping and encouraging others with their gifts, putting out a hand if needed, and being a shoulder to cry on. I'm not saying let people abuse your goodness. Learn to set limits. What I am saying is that we are all sisters and brothers of the earth. No matter what our differences are, there are many more similarities. I believe we all chose to come here and do these lessons, and sometimes they are not easy ones to learn. If your friend is having trouble, give her a kind word or take her to lunch. Tell her she can call you if needed, or send her a card or some flowers. If you make this part of your life, I can guarantee that if you are going through a rough time, someone will come to your aid.

A joyful summary

I hope this book will help you on your quest to becoming a happy, healthy lesbian. This is a new millennium, full of the promise of equality for us all, and I wish you the brightest, most wonderful future you could ever imagine.

Love and the very best to you in all ways,

Tracey Stevens

Bibliography

Want to get there fast?

You can find live links to these books and websites at

http://www.amazingdreamspublishing.com/hlbiblio.html

Reference Books

Bagemihl, Bruce, *Biological Exuberance: Animal Homosexuality and Natural Diversity*, New York: St Martin's Press, 1999.

Bass, Ellen; Davis, Laura, *The Courage to Heal, A Guide for Women Survivors of Child Sexual Abuse*, New York: Harper & Row, Publishers, 1994.

Boswell, John, *Same-Sex Unions in Premodern Europe*, New York: Villiard Books, a Division of Random House, Inc., 1994.

Bradshaw, John, *Home Coming, Reclaiming and Championing Your Inner Child*, New York: Bantam Books, 1992.

Brown, Mildred L.; Rounseley, Chloe Ann, *True Selves: Understanding Transsexualism*, San Francisco: Jossey-Bass Publishers, 1996.

Davis, Laura, *The Courage to Heal Workbook, For Women and Men Survivors of Child Sexual Abuse*, New York: Harper & Row, Publishers, 1990.

Grabhorn, Lynn, *Excuse Me, Your LIFE Is Waiting*, Virginia: Hampton Roads Publishing Company, Inc., 2000.

Koop, C. Everett, M.D., *Dr. Koop's Self-Care Advisor*, California: Time Life Medical, The Health Publishing Group, 1996.

Komaroff, Anthony L., M.D., *Harvard Medical School Family Health Guide*, New York: Simon & Schuster, 1999.

Masters, William H.; Johnson, Virginia E.; Kolodny, Robert C., Human Sexuality 4th Edition, New York: Harper Collins, 1992.

Miller, Neil, *Out of the Past, Gay and Lesbian History from 1869 to Present*, New York: Vintage Books, Division of Random House Books, 1995.

Murray, Raymond, *Images in the Dark: An Encyclopedia of Gays and Lesbians in Film and Video*, New York: Penguin Press, 1996.

Bleiler, David (Editor), TLA Video, *TLA Film and Video Guide: A Discerning Film Lovers Guide*, New York: Griffin Trade Paperback, St. Martin's Press, 1999.

Russell, Paul, *The Gay 100, A Ranking of the Most Influential Gay Men and Lesbians, Past and Present*, New Jersey: Citadel Press Book, published by Carol Publishing Group Edition, 1995.

Sisley, Emily L., M.D.; Harris, Bertha, *The Joy of Lesbian Sex*, New York: Simon & Schuster, 1977.

Stone, Merlin, *When God Was a Woman*, New York: Dorset Press, 1976.

West, Celeste, *A Lesbian Love Advisor*, Pennsylvania: Cleis Press, 1989.

Westheimer, Ruth, M.D., *Sex For Dummies*, California: IDG Books Worldwide Inc., 1995.

Internet Articles

Can Animals Be Gay? New Book Stirs Debate
By Steve Grant
Posted by USA on March 24, 1999
Hartford Courant, March 23, 1999
285 Broad St., Hartford, CT, 06115
http://nz.com/NZ/Queer/OUT/news/1999_03/290.html

Queer Creatures
From *New Scientist,* August 7, 1999
http://www.newscientist.com/ns/19990807/queercreat.html

**Just the Facts About Sexual Orientation & Youth:
A Primer for Principals, Educators & School Personnel**
GLSEN (Gay, Lesbian and Straight Education Network)
http://www.glsen.org/templates/resources/record.html?section=15
&record=424

**Symbols of the Gay, Lesbian, Bisexual, and Transgender
Movements**
Featured on the Lambda.org website
Charles Edward Riffenburg IV, Copyright 1998
http://www.lambda.org/symbols.htm

Understanding the Gay Agenda
Viewer's Notes and Historical Comments About Anti-Gay
Propaganda by Brad L. Graham, Copyright 1993, The Privacy
Rights Education Project (PREP), St. Louis, Missouri
http://www.prepstl.org/gayagenda.html

**Summary of States, Cities, and Counties Which Prohibit
Discrimination Based on Sexual Orientation**
Lambda Legal Defense and Educational Fund
Copyright 2002, Lambda Legal Defense and Educational Fund
http://lambdalegal.org/cgibin/pages/documents/record?record=217

Online Exhibition "Do you remember when?"
United States Holocaust Memorial Museum
http://www.ushmm.org/doyourememberwhen/

Resources

Want to get there fast?
You can find live links to these books and websites at
http://www.amazingdreamspublishing.com/hlbiblio.html

Helping your family understand:

Parents, Families and Friends of Lesbians and Gays (PFLAG)
1726 M Street, NW, Suite 400, Washington, DC 20036,
202-467-8180
PFLAG'S easy-to-use website has lots of information
and lists local chapters by state: http://www.pflag.org/
email: info@pflag.org
With 488 chapters reaching over 80,000 households, Parents,
Families and Friends of Lesbians and Gays (PFLAG) helps gay,
lesbian, bisexual, and transgendered (GLBT) people, their families
and friends, through support, education, and advocacy. PFLAG's line
of publications addresses a variety of support and educational issues
for both GLBT people and allies. Their publications help prepare
families and friends for the challenges of supporting GLBT loved
ones. PFLAG's mission promotes the health and well-being of gay,
lesbian, bisexual and transgendered persons, their families and friends
through: support, to cope with an adverse society; education, to
enlighten an ill-informed public; and advocacy, to end discrimination
and to secure equal civil rights. PFLAG provides opportunities for
dialogue about sexual orientation and gender identity, and acts to
create a society that is healthy and respectful of human diversity.

Books to help your parents, family, and friends:

*Beyond Acceptance: Parents of Lesbians and Gays Talk About
Their Experiences* by Carolyn Welch Griffin, Marian J. Wirth,
Arthur G. Wirth, Brian McNaught, December 1997, St. Martin's
Press; ISBN: 0312167814

Coming Out As Parents: You and Your Homosexual Child
by David K. Switzer, September 1996, Westminster John Knox
Press; ISBN: 0664256368

*Is It a Choice?: Answers to 300 of the Most Frequently Asked
Questions About Gay and Lesbian People* by Eric Marcus,
June 1999, Harper San Francisco; ISBN: 006251623X

My Child Is Gay: How Parents React When They Hear the News
by Bryce McDougall (Editor), October 1998, Allen & Unwin;
ISBN: 1864486589

*Outing Yourself: How to Come Out As Lesbian or Gay to Your
Family, Friends, and Coworkers* by Michelangelo Signorile,
June 1996, Fireside; ISBN: 0684826178

*Straight Parents, Gay Children: Inspiring Families to Live
Honestly and With Greater Understanding* by Robert A.
Bernstein, May 1999, Thunder's Mouth Press; ISBN: 1560252294

Organizations that fight for our rights:

GLAAD (Gay & Lesbian Alliance Against Defamation)
http://www.glaad.org/
The Gay & Lesbian Alliance Against Defamation (GLAAD) is
dedicated to promoting and ensuring fair, accurate, and inclusive
representation of individuals and events in all media as a means of
eliminating homophobia and discrimination based on gender identity
and sexual orientation.

GLAAD Atlanta, 159 Ralph McGill Blvd., Ste. 506,
Atlanta, GA 30308, 404-614-3700

GLAAD Kansas City, 1509 Westport Road,
Kansas City, MO 64111, 816-756-5991

GLAAD Los Angeles, 5455 Wilshire Blvd., Suite 1500
Los Angeles, CA 90036, 323-933-2240

GLAAD New York, 248 West 35th St., 8th Floor,
New York, NY 10001, 212-629-3322

GLAAD San Francisco, 1360 Mission St., Suite 200,
San Francisco, CA 94103, 415-861-2244

GLAAD Washington, DC, 1700 Kalorama Road, NW,
Washington, DC 20009, 202-986-1360

GLSEN (Gay, Lesbian and Straight Education Network)
http://www.glsen.org
"GLSEN is the leading national organization fighting to end anti-gay bias in K-12 schools."
121 West 27th St., #804, New York, NY 10001-6207

Hate Crime Network - a project of LAMBDA GLBT Community Services
http://www.HATE-CRIME.net
The National Hate Crimes Hotline, 800-686-HATE
The Hate Crime Network (HCN) was created by a team of experienced hate crime victim advocates who know the importance of hate crime laws, recovery services, and improved police response. But they also know that for the thousands of Americans affected by hate crimes each year, none of that matters if they can't tell anyone what happened. Survivors of bias incidents often say that they fear reporting to the police or that they simply don't know where to turn for help. The national Hate Crime Network (HCN) gives hate crime victims a chance to tell someone what happened to them. And it gives all of us the opportunity to tell hate crime victims that they are not alone.

LAMBDA GLBT Community Services
http://www.lambda.org/
P.O. Box 31321, El Paso, TX 79931-0321, 208-246-2292
"Nonprofit, gay/lesbian/bisexual/transgender agency dedicated to reducing homophobia, inequality, hate crimes, and discrimination by encouraging self-acceptance, cooperation, and nonviolence."

National Lesbian & Gay Journalists Association
http://www.nlgja.org/
P.O. Box 423048, San Francisco, CA 94142, 415-905-4690
A professional organization for gay and lesbian media employees.

National Gay and Lesbian Task Force (NGLTF)
http://www.ngltf.org/
1700 Kalorama Road NW, Washington, DC 20009-2624,
202-332-6483

The National Gay and Lesbian Task Force works to eliminate prejudice, violence, and injustice against gay, lesbian, bisexual, and transgender people at the local, state, and national level. As part of a broader social justice movement for freedom, justice, and equality, NGLTF is creating a world that respects and celebrates the diversity of human expression and identity where all people may fully participate in society.

Political Research Associates
1310 Broadway, Suite 201, Somerville, MA 0214, 617-666-5300
http://www.publiceye.org/
Monitors right-wing groups, with extensive research on homophobic movements.

Where to go for help if you've been sexually abused:

The Rape, Abuse & Incest National Network (RAINN)

635-B Pennsylvania Ave. SE, Washington, DC 20003,
1-800-656-4673
http://www.rainn.org/

RAINN is a nonprofit organization based in Washington, D.C. that operates a national hotline for survivors of sexual assault. The hotline offers free, confidential counseling from anywhere in the country. You can call the RAINN hotline 24 hours a day at 1-800-656-HOPE, or you can locate a crisis center near you by using their search function on their website. RAINN is provided as a service for survivors who cannot reach a rape crisis center through a local call. Currently, the majority of the country is a toll call away from a rape crisis center. Many of these long distance callers are being abused by someone in their own household and thus can't utilize a service that will appear on a phone bill.

Online support for lesbians of domestic partner abuse; childhood psychological, physical or sexual abuse; rape and hate crimes:

Rainbow Hope
http://www.rainbowhope.org
We support lesbians who were abused (psychological, physical or sexual) in their childhoods, who were raped, who were victims of hate crimes or of domestic violence. This site was created so that we could share our experiences, grief, hopes, struggles and dreams. We wanted to create a space where women could be themselves without the fear of being judged because of sexual orientation issues. We hope that we can provide you with a safe place to finally be able to be completely yourself.

Breaking The Silence
http://t.webring.com/hub?ring=survivors
Open to everyone; age, gender, background irrelevant. Survivors of sexual and gender violence; rape; sexual abuse, harassment; FGM; and G/L/B/T hate crimes. Most are against women by men, but we don't seek to exclude male survivors or victims of female assailants. Sites in the web ring are by or about survivors and most include resources or inspiration in coping with surviving. Our motto is: "Work for survival, and refuse to keep the secrets of the crimes we have suffered." By sharing our pain, we are sharing our strengths.

Lesbian-friendly places to buy books, videos, music, toys, and do other stuff

Books, videos, and music

InsightOutBooks.com
http://www.insightoutbooks.com/
InsightOutBooks.com is the first book club ever created specifically for LGBT readers, family, and friends. InsightOut is a place where

the diversity of voices within the LGBT community will be heard, shared, and celebrated.

The Lesbian Shopper
http://www.lesbianshopper.com
"Your one-stop shop for lesbian books, magazines, movies, classifieds and more. We've taken the work out of scouring the Internet for great lesbian products and items by creating a site of nothing but the best in Lesbian everything: reading, watching, listening, wearing and more!"

TLA Video
TLA Entertainment Group, 234 Market Street, Philadelphia, PA 19106, 215-733-0608
http://www.tlavideo.com

Store Locations:
South Street-Society Hill, 517 S. 4th Street, Philadelphia, PA 19147, 215-922-3838

Chestnut Hill, 7630 Germantown Ave., Philadelphia PA 19118, 215-248-4448

RittenhouseSquare, 1520 Locust Street, Philadelphia, PA 19102, 215-735-7887

Bryn Mawr, 763 Lancaster Avenue, Bryn Mawr, PA 19010, 610-520-1222

Art Museum, 1808 Spring, Garden Street, Philadelphia, PA 19130, 215-751-1171

West Village, Manhattan, 52-54 West 8th Street, New York, NY 10001, 212-228-8282

Toys, safer sex items, and other stuff for us

Good Vibrations
http://www.goodvibes.com/
e-mail: goodvibe@well.com
Good Vibrations is a women-owned and women-operated cooperative

which has been promoting sexual health and pleasure since 1977. From a great antique vibrator online museum to toys for the new millennium, Good Vibrations has it all. Books, audio, video, and even a section to "Get Off Cheap" are included in their great website.

Good Vibrations San Fransisco, 1210 Valencia Street
(@ 23rd Street), San Francisco, CA 94110, 415-974-8980

Good Vibrations Berkeley Store, 2504 San Pablo Avenue
(@ Dwight), Berkeley, CA 94702, 510-841-8987

To order a catalog by phone, call: 800-289-8423

Toys in Babeland
http://www.babeland.com
email:mailorder@babeland.com
Toys in Babeland is the famously fun lesbian owned, women run adult toy store in Seattle, New York and online at Babeland.com. Find the gear, guidance and inspiration for a satisfying love life with the help of their staff educators. Visitors to Seattle and New York should check out the events listings on their website for their unique instore workshops: "Babeland University".

New York, Toys in Babeland, 94 Rivington Street
(between Orchard and Ludlow),
NewYork, NY 10002, 212-375-1701

Seattle, Toys in Babeland, 707 E. Pike Street,
Seattle, WA 98122, 206-328-2914.

To order a catalogue by phone: 800-658-9119

Internet info, hosting, and searching

A lesbian introduction to the Internet
http://www.lesbian.org/internet-guide/guide.html

Lesbian-Friendly Web Hosting
kryss.com
http://www.kryss.com/
"Looking for award-winning website design, a webmaster to help

186

you maintain your site, an e-commerce package that ROCKS, or a great place to get low-cost affordable web hosting? At kryss.com, we aim for 100% Customer Satisfaction. We have lightning fast, reliable servers, connections, service, and support. We are also well-known for including more features with our virtual hosting package than many hosts charging two to five times more. Check out our Hosting Comparison page to see why you should choose kryss.com as your web presence provider."

Search the "Queer" Internet
http://www.rainbowquery.com/

Free Nonpornographic Lesbian E-Cards
http://www.amazingdreamspublishing.com/ecards.html

How to find other lesbians with similar interests

Lesbian Mailing Lists
http://www.lesbian.org/lesbian-lists/index.html
Huge listing of women-only, Sapphic, lesbian centered, or similarly defined mailing lists. From Artistic Dykes and GranolaGrrls, to Babydykes and The Gillian Anderson Estrogen Brigade, this list has it all.

Lesbian Chat Galore (LCG)
http://www.4wmn.com/
LCG is one of the most popular online meeting places for the lesbian, bisexual, and transgender community. You can interact, chat, and make use of the free personals, pen pal, and matchmaking systems.

Other books by Tracey Stevens

Lesbian Sex Tips: A Guide for Anyone Who Wants
to Bring Pleasure to the Woman She (Or He) Loves

By Tracey Stevens & Kathy Wunder, nonfiction, ISBN 0-9719628-2-0
This manual is an excerpt from *How To Be A Happy Lesbian: A Coming Out
Guide*, and it contains more than just sexual tips. Included are illustrations
and instructions on how to find the spots that please a woman most; advice
on romance and communication; plain talk about safer sex and how to protect
your partner and yourself; and pointers on passion and how to bring a woman
to orgasm. Filled with humor, this book is definitely not a dry "how-to"
manual. It was written for the benefit of all consenting adults who love
women.

Chalice of the Goddess

By Tracey Stevens, fiction, ISBN 0-9719628-4-7
Devon and her brother, Bilton, were born to a poor blacksmith and his wife
in France during the Lord's Year 1300. Devon came into this world with a
caul covering her face, a sure sign of clairvoyance and witchcraft. Madeline
Dartenmarth lives in a cliff castle in a nearby township called Ellisbeth.
Madeline speaks to angels and longs for a woman who is true of heart and
not just after money and power. Devon is terrified of her "dark gift" and
Madeline relies on her connection to the other side to help her tolerate her
hateful mother. Madeline and Devon are lesbian soulmates. If either one of
them knew the destiny they had chosen before their birth, they would never
stay together. Spiritual teachings by angels, telepathic communication with
animals, psychic gifts, and reincarnation, joined with a bawdy lesbian
romance . . . all injected with rollicking humor is the basis of this first
meeting of some of the modern-day Sandstone characters.

Above Faith, Beyond Fear: The Case of the Koolsicle Killer

By Tracey Stevens, fiction, ISBN 0-9719628-6-3
A serial killer is brutally murdering men in Sandstone, Florida, and Detective
Andrea Kickerson is hot on the trail. Andrea sees things others don't, but
refuses to admit that she is psychic. Andrea's lover, Candace Williams, is a
case manager for the chronically mentally ill. Candace works with her friend,
Daniell Harmon, and the two have their own theories about who the killer is
and why he is doing what he's doing.